THE GOVERNMENT
OF POLAND

ISBN 0–915145–96–0 (cloth)
ISBN 0–915145–95–2 (pbk)

Previously published by
Bobbs-Merrill as ISBN 0–672–60391–8 (pbk)

THE GOVERNMENT
OF POLAND

JEAN-JACQUES ROUSSEAU

*Translated, with an Introduction
and Notes, by*
WILLMOORE KENDALL

Preface by
HARVEY C. MANSFIELD, JR.

HACKETT PUBLISHING COMPANY
Indianapolis

The edition of Rousseau's works used
for this translation is
Oeuvres complètes de J. J. Rousseau,
(Paris: Chez Furne, 1835)

JEAN-JACQUES ROUSSEAU: 1712–1778

Cover design by Richard L. Listenberger
For further information, please address
Hackett Publishing Company, Inc.
P. O. Box 44937
Indianapolis, Indiana 46244-0937

99 98 97 96   3 4 5 6 7 8 9 10

Library of Congress Cataloging in Publication Data

Rousseau, Jean Jacques, 1712–1778.
The government of Poland.

Translation of: Considérations sur le gouvernement de Pologne.
Reprint. Originally published: Indianapolis:
Bobbs-Merrill, 1972. (Library of liberal arts)
Bibliography: p.
1. Poland—Politics and government. I. Title.
[JN6750.R6213 1985]   320.9438   85-5463
ISBN 0–915145–96–0
ISBN 0–915145–95–2 (pbk.)

The paper used in this publication meets the minimum requirements of
American National Standard for Information Sciences—Permanence of
Paper for Printed Library Materials, ANSI Z39.48-1984.

∞

CONTENTS

	Dedication	vi
	PREFACE	vii
	INTRODUCTION: How to read Rousseau's *Government of Poland*	ix
	THE GOVERNMENT OF POLAND	
I.	THE ISSUE POSED	1
II.	THE SPIRIT OF ANCIENT INSTITUTIONS	5
III.	THE FOREGOING APPLIED TO POLAND	10
IV.	EDUCATION	19
V.	THE RADICAL VICE	25
VI.	PROBLEM OF THE THREE ORDERS	27
VII.	MEANS OF MAINTAINING THE CONSTITUTION	31
VIII.	CONCERNING THE KING	48
IX.	SPECIFIC CAUSES OF ANARCHY	55
X.	ADMINISTRATION	62
XI.	THE ECONOMIC SYSTEM	67
XII.	THE MILITARY SYSTEM	79
XIII.	PLAN FOR STEP-BY-STEP PROMOTION FOR ALL MEMBERS OF THE GOVERNMENT	89
XIV.	ELECTING THE KING	101
XV.	CONCLUSION	110
	LIST OF WORKS CITED	117

DEDICATION

To Leo Strauss, the colleague and teacher
under whom, Willmoore often said, he put
himself to school again to learn what the
ancients and the moderns have to teach us.

NELLIE KENDALL

PREFACE TO THE 1985 REPRINTING

For students of political philosophy, three things of the first importance are to be found in Rousseau's *The Government of Poland* that amply justify the reprinting of Willmoore Kendall's excellent translation. The first is nationalism. Rousseau says on the first page that "one must know thoroughly the nation for which one is building," and he proceeds to prescribe for Poland's politics and constitution with a view always to the character of the Polish nation. Rousseau was the first political philosopher to prescribe in this manner by taking the nation as a given fact, to which politics must adjust, rather than as a product of politics, which legislators can remake. Modern nationalism is in essence this same fashioning of politics on the basis of a prepolitical fact, the nation — and thus owes its intellectual origin to Rousseau.

Second, we find Rousseau's conception of the legislator. To respect the given character of a nation, Rousseau's legislator must "move men's hearts," for example in the games they play as children, rather than coerce their souls. Instead of demanding the performance of virtues, the legislator should "choke off vices before they are born." This indirectness in legislation leads to the third noteworthy point, Rousseau's surprising caution and conservatism in *The Government of Poland* versus his radicalism in the *Social Contract*. In the former he says: "Never forget as you dream of what you wish to gain, what you might lose." In the *Social Contract,* to which he refers several times in this writing, he says in uncompromising words that "every legitimate government is republican." How can Rousseau's prudent advice to Poland be consistent with his insistence that only the best state is legitimate?

To raise this issue of theory and practice is the main purpose of Willmoore Kendall's introduction. His essay is still the best analysis of Rousseau's *The Government of Poland*. A citizen and a scholar himself, Kendall (who died in 1967) remains a vivid presence in his work and in the memories of his students and friends.

HARVEY C. MANSFIELD, JR.
Harvard University

INTRODUCTION
How to read Rousseau's
Government of Poland

"Jean-Jacques," writes Rousseau in his *Rousseau Passes Judgment on Jean-Jacques* (the last and most bitter of his writings about himself),

> devoted six months . . . first to studying the constitution of an unhappy nation [*i.e.*, Poland], then to propounding his ideas on the improvements that needed to be made in that constitution, all at the urging, reiterated with great stubbornness, of one of the first patriots of the nation in question, who made a humanitarian duty of the tasks he imposed.[1]

Rousseau, as he is likely to do when recounting an incident in his own life, is here mixing fact and fancy. First, he probably did undertake this final venture into political theory with some reluctance—in part because he had announced his intention to have done with political problems (his mind, in this the evening of his life, is increasingly filled with thoughts about *religion*), in part because he was determined to have

[1] *Oeuvres complètes de J. J. Rousseau,* (Paris: Chez Furne, 1835), vol. IV, p. 82.

ix

done with writing altogether (after the age of fifty, he seldom took pen in hand except for this or that polemic in defense of his reputation). One should also remember that Rousseau had made clear in *The Social Contract* [2] his "vocation" for the role of Legislator for any and every "unhappy nation" that might, in its hour of need, wish to avail itself of his wisdom. He had, indeed, already "legislated" for Corsica, in his *Projet de Constitution pour la Corse* (1765), and while one can imagine his having wanted some persuading by the Poles as regards his stipend, since he was invariably short of money, and about the delivery date of his manuscript, since he was, and thought of himself as being, undisciplined about his literary work, no one familiar with his life and personality could conceive of his actually saying "No" to an invitation to wrap himself, even momentarily, in the mantle of Solon. His lips may have been saying No, but his heart must have been saying Yes.

Second, while we know very little about Count Wielhorski, who "commissioned" the writing of the *Poland* (we do not, for example, possess the initial correspondence between him and Rousseau), and while we certainly have no reason to question his patriotism, his position as a leading Polish patriot, as we hear of it in Rousseau's version, is unsupported by evidence. All we know is that a Polish Convention sitting at Balia, in 1769, and without clear authority to act for Poland, resolved to request the advice of contemporary French political theorists as to the kind of constitution Poland should give itself if and when it found itself in control of its own destiny, and that Wielhorski was named as the Convention's *agent* for the relevant negotiations; there is no evidence that his role in Polish affairs was, or was likely to become, one of power and influence, certainly no evidence that he was in a position to name a Legislator for Poland.

Third, Rousseau, in point of fact, was only one of three political theorists whom Wielhorski put to work on Poland's constitutional problems, and not even the first of those three.

[2] Book II, Chapter X.

The Abbé Mably,[3] who was the first, completed his work so speedily that Rousseau saw, and took into account, what he had written before submitting his own manuscript. Moreover, Mably's proposals—Mably was not, at that time, inferior to Rousseau in point of reputation—seem to have received a certain amount of attention from participants in the then furious debate in Poland concerning constitutional problems; whereas Rousseau's book, to judge from the evidence readily available, went pretty much unnoticed.

But, fourth, and most importantly in understanding his intentions, Rousseau considerably exaggerates the amount of homework (six months of study) he did before writing his book. As he makes clear on the first page of his manuscript, he pretends to no knowledge of Poland beyond what he has picked up from a manuscript written, and placed in his hands, by Wielhorski himself (presumably the manuscript of the book, *The Ancient Constitution of Poland,* which in due course was published in London and, curiously enough, in French). Besides this information, Rousseau knew only what he might have picked up from the newspapers.

This fact alone should have caused Rousseau's critics to treat *The Government of Poland* with at least a certain minimum of caution, which, however, is nowhere to be found in the relevant literature: Rousseau, as we know him from his other writings, is above all a "demon" for homework—that is, a man who writes always out of an encyclopedic knowledge of the literature bearing upon the topic he has in hand. Only in the *Poland* do we find him insisting, if I may put it so, upon his ignorance; and only in the *Poland,* and in one of his later works, do we find him apologizing for his allegedly failing intellectual powers. One wonders that no critic has asked why,

[3] Gabriel Bonnot Mably was commissioned by Wielhorski to submit his suggestions for the reorganization of the Polish Constitution sometime early in 1770. He completed the first installment of his work in August of 1770 and the second in July of 1771. In general Mably called for a much more radical change in Polish political institutions than Rousseau felt to be necessary.

knowing so little about it, he was willing to write on Poland at all. How seriously should we take his statement that he is no longer, intellectually, the man he once had been? Similarly, should we not view with some skepticism his account, both in the passage I have cited and in the finished product itself, of the motivations that led him to write the book we have before us? This is not to say that Rousseau did not work hard on the book, which could not have been easy to write, but simply that the book and Rousseau's homework on the book are different matters, and that it would be difficult to point anywhere in the book to evidence that Rousseau's intelligence had at this time fallen on evil days; the *Poland* is certainly as shrewd and sharp as anything Rousseau has bequeathed to us.

One final point needs to be made before we understand Rousseau's intentions. Charles Hendel, an able Rousseau scholar, writes of the circumstances attending the composition of *The Government of Poland:* "A few years later," says Hendel in *Jean-Jacques Rousseau, Moralist,*

> the cause of liberty again drew him away from his own concerns and memories, when a call came, in 1771, from certain patriots in Poland, to be their legislator. He worked hard at this task and finished his [book] . . . the very next year, only to see it rendered impracticable by . . . the partition of Poland.[4]

We have already indicated some of our doubts concerning this account which Hendel simply accepts from Rousseau. But beyond the points already made above, Hendel's reference to "the cause of liberty" as the motivation that produced the *Poland* wants some thinking about, though not because it is gratuitous: Rousseau does, in the course of his argument, repeatedly refer to Poland's "freedom" as one of his central concerns. But the "freedom" in question is not, as Hendel's

[4] Charles W. Hendel, *Jean-Jacques Rousseau, Moralist* (London and New York: Oxford University Press, 1934), Volume II, p. 314.

"again" would suggest, the *liberté* of Rousseau's earlier political writings, which is the freedom of the *individual* over against his society and his government. The "freedom" of *The Government of Poland* is, quite simply, the freedom of the Polish people from foreign domination, that is, in the jargon of our own contemporary politics, "self-determination"; and even that is put forward not as a "cause," a principle applicable to all peoples everywhere and always; it is, specifically, the *Poles'* freedom, from, specifically, *Russian* domination. Nor is it true, as Hendel apparently would like us to believe, that the First Partition "rendered" Rousseau's proposals about Polish freedom "impracticable," since Rousseau must have known about the Partition before he submitted his manuscript to Wielhorski.[5] Furthermore, the *Poland* is, from first to last, clearly pessimistic about Poland's prospects for self-determination. Indeed, Rousseau tends to take it for granted that the Poles will, in due course, become Russian subjects. It would, in point of fact, be no exaggeration to say that on the deepest level *the* problem of the book, *as far as Polish affairs are concerned*, reduces itself to this: How can the Poles remain "free" even under a Russian occupation? And Rousseau's solution to that problem—let the Poles build their republic in their own hearts, beyond the reach of foreign swords—is not without interest in connection with Rousseau's motivation (of which I have spoken above, and will have more to say below) in addressing a book to Poland; he is, he says, attracted to the Poles precisely because he sees in them the capacity for being "free" in a very special, if paradoxical, sense of the word "free." To anticipate a little again, it helps explain his glorification, throughout his book, of Moses as the supreme Legislator, or Lawgiver: Moses' act of founding, by contrast with that of lesser Founders, formed a people able to maintain its identity, and thus its "freedom," even when scattered to the four winds and without a "State" or government of its own.

[5] C. E. Vaughan, *Jean-Jacques Rousseau: The Political Writings* (New York: John Wiley & Sons, 1962), pp. 391–394.

The last of the points I have made in the foregoing analysis cannot be overemphasized: Hendel clearly sees no problem, particularly no problem of "continuity," as regards the relation between *The Government of Poland* and even the more recent of Rousseau's other ventures in political theory. For Hendel, one might say, as also for the remaining handful of critics who have written on the *Poland* (let me note in passing that it is the least written about of Rousseau's political writings), the book is precisely what we might fairly have expected from the author of *The Social Contract*, given the invitation from a people "struggling to throw off its chains." And that, let us notice in fairness to Hendel, is just the impression that Rousseau, on the surface at least, seeks to convey in the book itself, where he misses no opportunity to refer back to the *Contract* for the "principles" whose validity the reader takes for granted as he proceeds with his argument.

I do not, as the reader will have guessed, think for a moment that we can leave it at that; indeed, my first obligation in writing this introduction—for readers who, presumably, approach the *Poland* for the first time, but are more or less familiar with *The Social Contract*—is to alert them to the emphases in the book that, on the face of it, come strangely from the pen that wrote "All men were born free, but are everywhere in chains." Item: We think of the Rousseau of the *Contract* as, above all, a *revolutionary*, prepared, out of hand, to declare all States illegitimate that do not meet the test of *his* "principles of political right," most especially that test of all tests, which is the supremacy of a "general will" from whose formation no individual is flatly excluded. Thus the first thing we should expect him to say to Poland, which concentrates all political power in the hands of an aristocracy and keeps most of its population in perpetual serfdom, is that it is illegitimate, a tyranny. But *The Government of Poland* does not, even by the remotest implication, strike any such note; far from claiming "freedom" for Poland's serfs, Rousseau counsels *against* their liberation within any foreseeable future, and he makes no mention of the "general will." Item: We think of the Rousseau of

The Social Contract as centrally preoccupied with, *inter alia*, the need for a "civil religion" as a cohesive force in any legitimate society. *The Government of Poland*, by contrast, avoids the topic of religion as if it belonged to the category of the unmentionable; one searches its pages in vain, for example, for any recognition of the fact that the country whose institutions he has under the knife happens to be a Roman Catholic country (though the Rousseau of *The Social Contract* certainly seemed to be saying that Roman Catholicism is incompatible with any defensible political order). Item: *The Social Contract* does not so much as mention education, and the educational "system," as a problem for political philosophy. In the *Poland*, by contrast, we are told at an early moment (Chapter Four, beginning) that education is *the* "important topic." Item: *The Social Contract*, in listing the several "kinds" of "law", conspicuously omits the "law of nature," or "natural law," thus breaking on a fundamental issue with the Great Tradition in political philosophy, and even with Locke, to whom Rousseau often points as one of his great teachers. In *The Government of Poland*, by contrast, we find Rousseau appealing to "natural law" as if it were a principle of long standing with him.[6] Item: *The Social Contract* certainly seems to be saying (on this point, at least, the spokesmen of the French Revolution were not demonstrably wrong when they styled themselves pupils of Rousseau) that man's political legacy from the past is a millstone about his neck—that he must, if he is to order his affairs rationally, wipe the slate clean and build his political institutions anew. Nothing in the *Contract* would prepare us for the theme, reiterated *ad libitum* in the *Poland*: Change nothing. Do not tamper with what you have. (Burke, who never missed an opportunity for excoriating Rousseau but was, presumably, unfamiliar with the *Poland*, was if anything less respectful than Rousseau here appears to be of the prescriptive claims of inherited institutions; would he, we wonder, had he read the *Poland*, have hailed Rousseau as the other great Tory of the century?)

[6] X, page 63. (WK transl.)

The question, once we lay the *Contract* and the *Poland* side by side, cannot be avoided: What, if we are to understand Rousseau and "place" him in the history of political philosophy, are we to make of such glaring discrepancies between two books by one and the same writer? Had Rousseau—as I perhaps seem to be wishing the reader to conclude—"changed his mind" in the interval between the two books, so that the repeated appeals in the *Poland* to the principles of the *Contract* are mere window dressing? That is indeed one answer to our questions, but not, let us notice, the only one possible, since at least two other answers readily suggest themselves: First, it could be argued that the Rousseau of the *Poland*, in order to ingratiate himself with those conservative Roman Catholic nobles who govern Poland, and to command their attention for his proposals, is willing to "pretend," for the purpose he has in hand, a kind of conservatism that certainly did not reflect his own deepest convictions—wherefore his sudden conversion to natural law, his astonishing silence about equality, etc. Perhaps, in order to carry the Polish nobles with him on certain matters of highest priority, Rousseau is prepared in the *Poland* to adjourn any differences he has with them on other matters. A second possibility is that the relation between *The Social Contract* and *The Government of Poland* is a reenactment (and probably a deliberate one, since Rousseau's mind is always filled with the classics) of the relation between Plato's *Republic* and Plato's *Laws*. Rousseau's *Contract*, like Plato's *Republic*, is a venture in "pure theory," in which the philosopher adjourns all considerations of "practicality" and seeks, for the questions he poses, answers that however impracticable are *true* universally and in all times; like Plato's *Republic*, Rousseau's *Contract* adumbrates a "pattern laid up in heaven." *The Government of Poland*, by contrast, like *The Laws* over against *The Republic*, brings the principles of *The Social Contract* "down to earth," and is thus a venture not in "pure theory" but in *practice;* it shows us what a putative Legislator, moving from certain more or less tacit principles on the level of pure theory, would recommend as "the thing to do" about politics at a specific time and place. As Eric Voegelin has ably demonstrated in the case of Plato, we should not expect a one-one correspondence between the theoretical principles and the practical recommendations—just as we should not hastily conclude, from apparent discrepancies between the principles and the practical proposals, that the latter do not flow consistently from the former. The proposals may embody all of the theoretical "model" that, given the circumstances of that time and place, can possibly be achieved there and then; or, an equally interesting possibility, they may seek to alter those circumstances in a way that, off in the future, will prepare the way for a further realization of the theoretical model.

I will content myself, for the tentative purposes of this Introduction, with directing the reader's attention to the question, How can we explain the discrepancies between Rousseau's *Contract* and his *Poland?* and to listing for him what seem to be the three most plausible answers that suggest themselves to a critic who has lived with the question for many years. The reader will, this critic believes, find the *Poland* all the more interesting if, as he reads it, he will attempt to decide for himself which of the three is the correct one.

This further word about our three possibilities (that Rousseau had changed his mind on some important questions, that Rousseau was being something less than open and candid with the Poles in the *Poland,* that the *Poland* is to the *Contract* what *The Laws* is to *The Republic*): if either of the first two possibilities is the correct one, we are entitled to read the *Poland* merely as what it purports to be, namely, an attempt (either by a "new" Rousseau, suddenly turned conservative, or by the "old" Rousseau prepared to "play games" with the Poles in order to carry them with him on certain major issues) to come to grips with the Poles' peculiar political problems and to point them along a path leading to a solution of those problems; that is, to read it as a prescription, written by Rousseau the political "physician," by way of ministering to the ills of Poland, the political "patient." If on the other hand the third possibility is correct, the *Poland* acquires an importance, for the history of political philosophy, that places it in an altogether different category, especially for those who think of Rousseau as one of the truly great political philosophers of modern times; it becomes a work that we must master in order to "round out" our understanding of Rousseau's whole political teaching. Put otherwise: If either of the first two possibilities is the correct one, the book stands or falls on its merits *as* "therapy" for the specific maladies of Poland. But if the third possibility is the correct one, if we must go to the *Poland* in order to learn the meaning, on the level of practice, of that one of the classics of modern political philosophy whose meaning remains most obscure—if the *Poland* is Rousseau's "last word" on the political plight not of Poland, but of modern man—it indeed becomes, for the student of political philosophy, a pearl of great price.

Again, if either of the first two possibilities is the correct one, the question of Rousseau's real reason for writing it remains on our hands, as does that of Rousseau's failure to do his homework before writing it: his treatment of Poland's *peculiar* problems, as the reader will see for himself, is at best superficial, hasty even; and, as we have seen, he looses the book upon the world at a moment when its chances of affecting those problems are infinitesimal. But if the third possibility is the correct one, if the book as a whole is directed not at Poland but at any and all countries more or less like Poland, if the book is a prescription not for Poland but for the territorially extensive modern nation-state as such, then Rousseau's motive in writing it becomes one that the student of political philosophy can guess for himself: Rousseau, who had made no secret of the fact that the *Contract* was a book that "needed to be done over," *had* to write it, since the alternative, intolerable for a philosopher with Rousseau's determination to have his impact upon the future of mankind, would have been to die without having revealed that part of his political teaching that would tell his future adepts what they must do. If either of the first two possibilities is the correct one, then the *Poland* is a book that means, quite simply, what it seems to say. But if the third possibility is the correct one, then the *Poland*—like most of the great works of modern political philosophy—becomes a venture in what Professor Leo Strauss has identified as "secret writing," and the critic's task thus becomes that of tearing from it its secret.

My answer to the question implied in the title of this Introduction cannot, then, be a simple one; rather, it must run in terms like the following. One can read the *Poland* in either of two ways: (a) as a book dealing centrally with Poland, and saying pretty much what it seems to say; or (b) as a book dealing centrally with the territorially extensive modern State, and saying much more than—and something different from—what it seems to say. Now, if we read it in the first of these two ways, we shall wish to fix our attention on those of Poland's problems that are peculiar to Poland, and thus on those aspects of Poland's political system that set it apart from this or that *other* emergent modern national State; while if we read it in the manner called for by the second approach, we shall wish to fix attention on those aspects of the Polish political system that it shares in common with those other states, and on what Rousseau proposes in connection with them.

Eighteenth-century Poland could indeed point to political maladies peculiar to herself, and these maladies were, in all conscience, sufficiently grave to challenge the capacities of any and all the political physicians she might have summoned, from France or wherever, to her bedside. I content myself with listing, and explicating in the briefest possible manner, at least the major ones.

a) Poland was, and had been for a long while at the time Rousseau wrote, *helpless militarily*, and thus at the mercy of her more powerful neighbors (Russia and Prussia, but Russia especially) as regards both her external and her internal affairs. Her inability to defend her frontiers, moreover, was not, or at least not primarily, a matter of insufficient natural resources in point of men and the sinews of war, but rather of the Poles' traditional jealousy of centralized authority. Poland was hamstrung by the unwillingness of the nobility to provide the central government with the funds it needed in order to maintain an adequate army; by its unwillingness to make available the necessary man power; above all, perhaps, by the nobles' refusal, symbolized by a laissez faire policy toward the existence of private armies at the command of local magnates, to concede to the central government that monopoly of force that had already revealed itself as the characteristic feature of the modern nation state.

b) Poland was, if not the unique, at least the extreme case of a nation state that, by mid-eighteenth century, had failed to develop a representative assembly capable of speaking, more or less authoritatively, as the "voice" of the Polish people. (England, of course, was the extreme case at the other end of the spectrum.) This "failure," which was the topic of a flood of "reformist" literature by Polish publicists throughout the eighteenth century, was attributed, by common consent, to two long established Polish political institutions, plus a more or less recent "perversion" of one of those institutions. First, the Polish Diet, in accordance with custom deeply rooted in centuries-old tradition and to the horror of Poland's "modernizers," maintained in its proceedings *the unanimity principle;* that is, it refused to go along with the apparently universal trend toward decisions by vote of the majority. Second, the delegates who composed the Diet (the "nonces") continued, again in accordance with long established custom, to arrive from their home constituencies with *imperative mandates;* which is to say their votes in the Diet were actually cast not by the nonces themselves but by the local "dietines" that elected them. Now, Poland's famed *liberum veto* had traditionally been synonymous with the unanimity principle (that is, it did not allow for legislation by "mere" majority rule). Indeed, no little confusion has been caused by the use of the term *liberum veto* to denote a perversion, or abuse, of the unanimity principle that presented itself at a relatively late moment in the history of the principle of majority rule and that, by carrying the logic of the unanimity principle on out to its unavoidable conse-

INTRODUCTION xxi

quences, had reduced Poland's national assembly to utter impotence. The nonces asserted, and in due course made good, a claim not merely to prevent any piece of legislation, or even any rule of parliamentary procedure, that any of them (whether in response to his imperative mandate or a personal whim) saw fit to oppose, but also to "veto" the deliberations themselves. That is to say, any nonce could, by pressing his veto, suspend the Diet altogether until his wishes, on an issue at stake, were met to his own satisfaction. (The first instance of such use of the veto occurred in 1669, and afterwards, during the reign of John Sobieski, 1674–1696, the precedent was employed with embarrassing regularity; half of the Diets convened during this period were not brought to a successful conclusion.) The two traditional institutions, the unanimity principle and the imperative mandate, would by themselves, of course, have sufficed to prevent the Polish Diet from becoming a *deliberative* assembly like, say, the House of Commons of the day. Because of the former, it was improbable that any decision could be taken; because of the latter, minds were already made up, so why deliberate? The two traditional institutions plus the perversion of the first deprived Poland, to all intents and purposes, of any national assembly at all, and thus invited the charge often heard in the eighteenth century that Poland had been reduced, or had reduced herself, to a state of *anarchy*.

c) Poland had refused to "follow the trend" on yet another matter; she had not provided herself with a hereditary monarchy; by long established custom *the Poles elected their kings*. Moreover, since on the face of it the choice of a new king, upon the death of his predecessor, did not lend itself to *imperative mandates*, the Polish nobles refused to entrust the king's election to the Diet. Rather, out of their imperturbable and rigorous anarchic logic, they insisted upon being present in the flesh at the elections and casting their votes personally—as well as upon tying the lucky man's hands with the famous Polish *pacta conventa*, or coronation oath. Suffice it to say that the latter left him as nearly naked of power as a man could conceivably be and still, without appearing ludicrous, call himself a king. The mind boggles as it attempts to conjure up the spectacle: *several hundred thousand* electors, each with a vote that, again by immemorial custom, was as "good" as that of every other man, assembled in one place to elect, and then politically emasculate—a king! To which we may add: the Polish throne, again by time-honored custom, was up for sale to the highest bidders, foreign and domestic, so that to ask a Polish noble to absent himself from elections, or to help create machinery for electing the king in some more "sensible" manner, was to ask him to renounce his proper share of the "take." He had traditionally preferred, down to the moment at which Rousseau writes the *Poland*, to be present. (With a hereditary monarchy we see the last of those perilous *interregna*, with their accompaniments of chaos and corruption.)

d) Unwilling as they were to provide themselves with a *constitutional* government capable of taking effective action in moments of national emergency, the Poles had formed the habit of relying upon an *extra*-constitutional device known as "Confederation." Once organized as a Confederation (Confederations, when they occurred, appear to have sprung up spontaneously and with amazing celerity) the Polish nobles did act by majority vote. One might say, indeed, that they had it both ways: a constitutional system built on the "golden right" of the *liberum veto*, too sacred to be sacrificed to majority rule, and extra-constitutional machinery capable, via temporary suspension of the *liberum veto*, of getting the country out of the major crisis which the constitutional system was sure to produce.

One readily sees first, why in the eyes of Poland's "modernizers"—encouraged (as modernizers usually are) by the intellectuals—all this called imperatively for "reform;" and second, the general shape that the modernizing program would necessarily take: make the monarchy hereditary, so that centralized power can accumulate, from generation to generation, in the hands of a dynasty which can be counted on to surround itself with the typical paraphernalia of the great modern state (extensive government departments, bureaucracies, what have you). Get rid, as a matter of course, of the perverted form of the *liberum veto*, which enables those mandated nonces to arrest the proceedings of the Diet. Abolish the Confederations, or rather render them unnecessary by giving up the unanimity principle, so that the king will be able to deal with a Diet reflecting the "will of the people" and know, from the way the winds are blowing in the Diet, where he stands and what he must do about it if he is to accomplish "great things" (foreign conquests? colonies abroad? what have you?). Abolish, above all, the imperative mandate and so wear down the power of those pestiferous local assemblies, so that the executive authority need no longer confront parliamentarians for whom all the important issues are "non-negotiable." Finally, let Poland provide herself, like other countries, with a regular army capable of making Poland's power felt, in international affairs, at least in proportion to her resources (and, if it be a good army, perhaps even more than in proportion to her resources). One readily sees, too, why it made sense for the modernizers to import (as Wielhorski was authorized to do) a little *expertise* from foreign parts and especially, since French political theory was "riding high," from that most modern of modern nations, France. The experts could be counted on to back up the reformers and strengthen their hand (though, one suspects, they should have known better than to call on Rousseau, whom they might easily have identified as a man unlikely to play their game).

Rousseau, as the reader will see for himself, does not play their game. He does, to be sure, take up one by one the alleged maladies of Poland as we have just listed them and does, in each case, offer a sort of solution. But in each case (this entirely apart from the general counsel to make as few changes as possible) he either takes sharp issue with the modernizers or gives to their proposal a "twist" that would produce a different result from that which they desire; or, almost but not quite the same thing, he "absorbs" their proposal into, or makes it serve the purposes of, a series of proposals for the political future of Poland that Poland's modernizers could only have regarded as "reactionary." Concretely, Rousseau urges the Poles, *mirabile dictu*, to retain their elective monarchy, contents himself with teaching them how to eliminate both the chaos and the corruption of the *interregna*, and then absorbs the whole business of electing the king into a general proposal for turning Polish society into a glorified civil service. (He also pauses to state, as vigorously and shrewdly as anyone has ever put it, the "case" against a hereditary monarchy—those pages alone might justify the book's claim to be included among the masterpieces of modern political philosophy.) Far from adopting the modernizers' proposal for a professionalized army (which, of course, centralized authority would be able to use, domestically, *against* those "pestiferous" local assemblies), Rousseau counters it with a proposal, modeled upon his beloved Switzerland, for a *citizens'* army, organized on the basis of local units, and far more likely, though Rousseau does not come out and say so, to check centralized authority than to expand it. Far, too, from going along with the modernizers' proposal to abolish the *imperative mandate*, Rousseau advises to keep it, and strengthen it, by having the dietines call the nonces on the carpet after each Diet and—ah! Jean-Jacques!—chop off their heads if even in the smallest particular they have disobeyed their instructions. Only on the *liberum veto* does he "go along in order to get along," and even here he wants watching. His animus, clearly, is against majority rule, and what his advice boils down to is, in effect: Get rid of the *liberum veto*, but also keep it. Abolish it with respect to the day-to-day business of government, he says in what is surely of all his proposals the most impossible to apply in practice, but retain it for certain matters of "fundamental" importance—though with the understanding that the man who imposes his veto, and thus frustrates the will of his fellow-parliamentarians, shall appear in due course before a Tribunal, which must either reward him as his country's savior or have him executed as a public nuisance! In other words, keep the *liberum veto*, but see to it that men think twice before resorting to it. As for the Confederation, again Rousseau refuses to go along with the modernizers: the memory of it, especially that of the recent Confederation of Bar (to which he refers repeatedly), must be cherished, as well as the possibility of resorting to it in future moments of need—which, should the Poles follow Rousseau's counsel and retain even a modified *liberum veto*, are only too likely to occur.

Rousseau's principal methods of handling the problems that preoccupy the Polish modernizers, then, are either (a) to deny that they *are* problems, and so brush them aside, or (b) to offer solutions that bear scant evidence of his having paid much attention either to their workability or to their chances of adoption, or (c), if I may put it so, to talk about something else, which, as I have already intimated, is what he does, for the most part, throughout the book. From first to last, one might say—and I am still speaking as I promised to do, in abstraction from any "hanky-panky," that is, secret writing, on Rousseau's part—Rousseau is quietly taking issue with the Polish reformers, and with the countless eighteenth-century publicists who have ridiculed and scorned the Polish Constitution, on an issue that is logically prior to any and all issues having to do with Poland's form of government, namely: Does Poland *want* to be a modern nation state—like, for example, France and England? And if it does not want to be such a state, should it want to be? All other participants in the discussion are tacitly assuming that Poland (that is, the politically active Poles) does want to follow the major European "trends," and that, therefore, the Poles are behaving foolishly in not giving themselves a form of government, a centralized authority, that will enable them to do so. Don't try to be powerful, Rousseau bids them; don't try to be rich; don't envy other nations their great and teeming cities, their industry, their foreign trade, their theaters and opera houses, their fancy clothes: all that sort of thing will, even if you achieve it, only turn to ashes in your hands. Furthermore, he tacitly assumes throughout his argument that he has the rank and file of the Poles *with* him on this prior issue—that, if you like, he is saying things that they have been waiting for someone with a tongue in his head to say to them; and that the alleged "vices" of the Polish Constitution represent a clearheaded and intelligent choice on the part of the rank-and-file Poles, against the centralized authority that their intellectual betters are urging upon them, and are, therefore, not vices but *virtues*. Why? Because it is precisely these apparent vices that prevent the Poles from having within their reach the false goods that they might otherwise pursue. It is hardly too much to say that the *Poland* is an open and unabashed appeal over the heads of the very elite that has commissioned it to the hearts and minds of the Polish people themselves—or, failing that, to some future elite which, having displaced the modernizers, will embrace the national *ethos* that Rousseau spells out in what finally emerge as the key chapters of the book.

One further point, and I shall have done with the first of our two ways of reading *The Government of Poland*. Just to the extent that Rousseau, in his overall argument, shifts attention from the alleged vices of the Polish Constitution to the national *ethos* he would like (as the case may be) to reinforce or to inculcate among the Poles, the book ceases, as I have tried to prepare the reader to expect it to, to be a book addressed to Poland and a future Polish elite. And, in doing so, it becomes, *mutatis mutandis*, a book addressed to all large nation states (all of them, he insists, are "hastening to their doom") and to a future elite in each of them which, after the inevitable disaster that awaits them, will teach their people to turn their backs on false goods, and to adopt political institutions appropriate to the pursuit of the genuine goods embodied in the way of life that Rousseau urges upon the Poles. But that leads us into the *Poland* as a venture in "secret writing," that is, it leads us to consider the *Poland* as a work that is apparently addressed to the Poles but is actually intended for a much wider audience, encompassing all those who find themselves unwilling participants in the modern, territorially extensive political regime.

Is there indeed a second possible reading of *The Government of Poland* that (a) places it in the category of "secret writing," and (b) makes of it a book that we must master if we are to arrive at a full understanding of Rousseau's political teaching and of, *inter alia*, *The Social Contract* itself? As the reader already knows, I believe the correct answer to the question to be "yes." But within the limitations of this Introduction, I can hardly do more than scratch the surface of the problems that our book poses when approached on the assumption that it says something different from, or something more than, it seems to say. The most I can hope to do is to give some illustrations of the sort of teaching that, though demonstrably present in the *Poland*, is in one way or another so handled as to escape the notice of the ordinary, casual, or hasty reader, and so convince the reader that the book requires the most careful kind of "close reading," that is, textual analysis. Not more than that, if only because, first, the *Poland* as a venture in "secret writing" is inseparable from *The Social Contract*, so that one must constantly weave back and forth between the earlier work and the later one in order to fully understand either of the books and, second, because I must pause to say a word about certain favorite techniques which Rousseau uses when he wishes to get across, to the careful reader for whom he is really writing, a point which he would prefer to be "lost" on most readers. These are not the techniques that Leo Strauss has ascribed to Machiavelli and Locke; they cannot be, because Rousseau resorts to them for a reason entirely different from that of Machiavelli or Locke. Machiavelli and Locke conceal their meaning because, to use Professor Strauss' terms, they are "cautious" men, who wish to say "shocking" things without bringing upon themselves the consequences of a reputation for entertaining "shocking" beliefs. Rousseau, by contrast, is by no means a cautious writer in that sense. Locke, for instance, would have regarded him as bold to the point of rashness; witness, for example, Rousseau's repeated open challenge to the prevailing religious orthodoxy of his day.

Rousseau—so at least this critic has come to believe after many years of poring over his writings—resorts to "secret writing" for a single and intimately personal reason, namely, to distract attention from any idea or proposal that might lay him open to ridicule, or that, in his own view, was not worth pressing upon his contemporaries (whom he had written off as hopeless), but *was* worth handing along to posterity. Put otherwise: More than any other political philosopher one can name, more even, I think, than Hobbes, Rousseau was convinced that he "knew all the answers," and that his were the answers that mankind would one day be driven to adopt. But, he was equally convinced that his "answers" were without relevance to the age in which he lived (unless, perhaps, in Geneva and Corsica and, just possibly, in Poland); and, at the same time, proud and sensitive man that Rousseau was, he was quite unwilling to accept, much less invite, a reputation for impracticality, or absurdity, or "utopianism." When, therefore, we find him concealing something—as, on the record, he successfully concealed what a careful reading will show to be the major proposal he had to make as a political philosopher—the first thing we notice is that it is something that his contemporaries would have deemed too foolish to be worth discussing, that is, the notion of giving up the large nation state for another form of polity.

Let me come a little closer to the point by spelling out that last remark. The central theme of *The Social Contract*, *the* idea that, now in one form and now in another, turns up again and again in the course of the argument, is the idea that man can be "moral" and "free" only in a self-contained community small enough to enable the citizens to meet and deliberate together in an assembly; that only in such a community are man's "chains," his "bondage," capable of being "justified," because only in such a community is it possible for the citizens to arrive at a "general will"; that any other form of political organization, above all the territorially extensive modern state, is *ipso facto* "illegitimate." That idea, along with the unavoidable implication that man, if he had his senses about him, would write off the modern state as an intolerable tyranny, fairly cries up at you out of the book—*if* you are prepared to take notice of it and treat it seriously. How explain the fact, then, that not one critic in a hundred who has written on Rousseau attributes that idea to *The Social Contract* as its central teaching, and that even the one critic who does is well nigh certain to sweep it aside as an "anachronism" on Rousseau's part, well nigh certain, that is to say, *not* to take it seriously. How explain the fact that though the number of critics who have "refuted" *The Social Contract* is legion, no critic comes to mind who has come to grips with that idea, and torn *it* to pieces? The only possible answer, I think, is that Rousseau has, with breath-taking artistry, so handled the idea that, in the very act of insisting upon it, he leads the reader's attention away from it, and sees to it that it will go unnoticed—as, on the record (I repeat), it for the most part has. One of Rousseau's techniques for concealing something, then, is that of making it simultaneously obvious and (for most readers) invisible.

In *The Government of Poland* Rousseau continues his attack on the typical form of the modern political regime, but he does so now in order to call for a return to what he conceives to be ancient virtue rather than to extemporize the conditions necessary for the formation of the "general will." In a sense, the *Poland* can be read as perhaps the last and certainly one of the most significant rehearsals of a theme that had absorbed French and English writers throughout the seventeenth and eighteenth centuries. The prevailing theme of the work is that of "Ancients vs. Moderns," and the book is characterized by Rousseau's continual confrontation of modern political and cultural practice with what he considers to be the superior modes and orders of Rome, Sparta, and Israel. He would have the Poles "establish a republic in their own hearts" that would effectively set them apart from their European contemporaries and would restore to them a sense of the healthier bonds of association enjoyed by the ancient polities. As he says, the key problem of devising a constitution for Poland (and, should we not infer, the central problem in founding an appropriate regime for any of the modern peoples?) is the task of raising contemporary man "to the pitch of the souls of the ancients." [7] The *Poland*, then, can be taken as a kind of provisional model for the grander program of refounding the nation-state along lines prescribed by the study of the ancients.

Poland, according to Rousseau, is confronted with the opportunity of forming for a large body of people dispersed over a wide area a government that may yet avoid the seemingly chronic despotism of other modern states. But this can be accomplished only by making the Poles into a tightly closed society with respect to the influence of other European regimes; and, above all, it can only be accomplished if the Poles are made to become so dependent upon one another that they come to feel they cannot exist apart from their unique political life. In this way the Polish citizen can be imbued with a sense of piety towards his native land and be made to feel a healthy repugnance for the cosmopolitan habits of the degenerate modern European. The Rousseau of the *Poland* seems simply to identify patriotism with virtue; consequently, he feels that to raise the souls of Polish citizens to the dignity of ancient virtue it is sufficient merely to diminish personal individuality by inculcating in the Poles an all-consuming devotion to the political order. Furthermore, it is Rousseau's contention that freedom is intimately connected with the kind of virtue he is describing in the *Poland;* and thus, somehow, true liberty is to be achieved only through the form of total government which he is proposing.

Rousseau indeed is proposing in the *Poland* a radically paradoxical, though by no means a totally new notion of freedom. Liberty, he says, is a food for strong stomachs, and it can only be attained as the result of a prior act of establishing rather harsh and extensive restraints:

I laugh at those debased peoples that let themselves be stirred up by agitators, and dare to speak of liberty without so much as having the idea of it; with their hearts still heavy with the vices of slaves, they imagine that they have only to be mutinuous in order to be free. Proud, sacred liberty! If they but knew

[7] III, pages 11–12. (WK transl.)

her, those wretched men; if they but understood the price at
which she is won and held; if they but realized that her laws are
stern as the tyrant's yoke is never hard, their sickly souls, the
slaves of passions that would have to be hauled out by the roots,
would fear liberty a hundred times as much as they fear servitude.
They would flee her in terror, as they would a burden about to
crush them.[8]

What needs to be restrained so that liberty may flourish
are, first of all, those selfish and private attachments of modern
man that cause division in society. More specifically, it is
above all the passion of acquisitiveness, which must be rooted
out from the hearts of men and replaced by the desire for
honor. Honor in turn is a monopoly of the state; Rousseau
would deny all avenues to glory except those that lead to the
service of the state. The Poles should follow the example of
the Romans and spurn all luxurious acquisitions as being inherently degrading; they should discourage commerce with other
countries and foster a frugal but self-sufficing agrarian econ-
omy. The trouble with modern European man, as Rousseau insists throughout the *Poland*, is that the failure of contemporary
legislators to provide him with institutions that promote a
fully politicized existence leaves him free to pursue—indeed
forces him to pursue—the divisive ends dictated by private interests. In view of this increasingly desperate situation, the
only way to prepare man for good legislation is by a prior
founding of unique "national institutions" that will so fill up
the horizon of his interests that he will have no opportunity
for creating private ends. As for the nature of Rousseau's envisaged ethos, he seems to say that almost anything will do as
long as it serves to promote a distinctively national character.

You must maintain or revive (as the case may be) your
ancient customs and introduce suitable new ones that will also
be purely Polish. Let these new customs be neither here nor there
as far as good and bad are concerned; let them even have their

[8] VI, pages 29–30. (WK transl.)

bad points; they would, unless bad in principle, still afford this advantage: they would endear Poland to its citizens, and develop in them an instinctive distaste for mingling with the peoples of other countries.[9]

It becomes more and more clear as one reads the *Poland* that Rousseau identifies the viciousness of the moderns with a certain randomness in the pattern of their lives. His notion of virtue, then, involves simply the replacement of "random man" with the kind of person whose life is ordered by some consistent purpose. This kind of person is the citizen or the completely public man; and it is the business of the state, or, more properly, it is the business of the founder of the state to see to it that the citizen passes every waking moment within institutions that will insure his constant attention to public affairs. To put it another way, for Rousseau the random life is slavery because it is constantly subject to the vicissitudes of the moment, whereas even under the most authoritarian regime the genuine citizen enjoys a superior freedom by virtue of his sense of purpose. Apart from being grounded in an intense piety toward the fatherland, Rousseau's notion of virtue is almost without content. Throughout the *Poland* he holds up the example of Sparta as the ancient regime most worthy to be emulated for the hardihood and simplicity of its citizens, but most of all for the unparalleled devotion to the state which was exemplified in its heroes from the time of Lycurgus onwards.

On the surface, at least, Rousseau's attack on the moderns may seem to be directed against what he sees as an all-pervasive egoism among contemporary man, and his model regime may recommend itself as a more noble polity based, as it seems to be, on unselfish motives of corporate piety. Rousseau certainly attempts to give the impression that he is urging a redirection of man's interest from the inherently base to the inherently noble. But if he is successful in conveying this impression, it is only because he very skillfully suppressed some

[9] III, page 14. (WK transl.)

of the more questionable implications of his teaching on virtue and freedom.

For example, Rousseau says nothing or next to nothing about the role of the Church in Polish affairs, and his silence on this point is more obtrusive in view of his many admonitions to preserve the traditional institutions of the country. Certainly we must suppose that Rousseau recognized the central place of religion in the lives of the Poles, and certainly we must credit him with realizing the difficulties posed by the Church's authority for the working out of his political model. How indeed can the citizen be expected to maintain a pure allegiance to the secular regime, as Rousseau would expect him to, when at the same time he is allied to the Church, which claims a superior authority over the individual conscience?

When faced with the same problem in *The Social Contract*, Rousseau gave the unequivocal answer that the state must create its own national religion in order to safeguard its claim to absolute obedience from the citizen.[10] In the *Poland*, however, the problem is never raised in the explicit manner of the earlier work. Instead, Rousseau chooses to drop the notion of a national religion and to severely limit the Church's influence by more indirect and subtle measures. Aside from a proposal regarding a rather insignificant administrative reform, Rousseau's only advice to the Poles on the issue of religion is imbedded in the context of his plans for a comprehensive system of state-controlled education. It would be wise, Rousseau suggests, to eliminate priests from the schools and to restrict the job of teaching to those who have entered upon a career in the state bureaucracy.[11] One may suspect that here is an instance of "secret writing" on Rousseau's part. The point he seems to be making might very well be ignored by the Poles, the immediate audience of this work, but a reader attentive to the implications of this recommendation—especially, we might add, a reader who is familiar enough with *The Social Contract*

[10] Cf. *The Social Contract*, Book IV, Chapter VIII.
[11] IV, page 20. (WK transl.)

to be sensitive to any change which Rousseau may now make on the teaching of that work—would quite likely seize upon Rousseau's suggestions on education as a new method for undermining the influence of religion in political life. Whereas the Rousseau of *The Social Contract* would replace revealed religion with some form of national moral creed, the Rousseau of the *Poland* prefers the more oblique strategy of leaving the Church pretty much to itself while quietly eliminating its hold on the schools. One might speculate, however, that the ultimate effect of the different strategies, if they are practiced successfully, would be the same: in either case the authority of religion will be eliminated, and the political order will be made absolute. By forcing the priests out of the schools the way is cleared for the purely nationalistic curriculum that Rousseau envisages as the first step in the process of radically politicizing the youth of the country.[12] Within a few generations religion will have ceased to be a significant part of Polish life, and subsequently its institutional structures will have become atrophied. Thus there will eventually be no voice to claim a "higher" law over against the laws of the political order.

The case against a higher authority is conveyed by Rousseau with an extraordinary degree of reserve, but the implications of his proposals force one to see the attack on revealed religion as one of the crucial features of the *Poland*. Similarly it should become obvious for the attentive reader that the work is also a veiled attack on the classical tradition of political philosophy, inasmuch as that tradition points to a source of right, *i.e.*, the "natural law" or, simply, "philosophy," which is of greater authority than the laws of any particular regime. There is no place in Rousseau's scheme of education for either religion or philosophy—both of these activities are implicitly excluded by the tightly closed curriculum that he proposes. These considerations should lead us to recognize an important qualification in his enthusiastic and, seemingly, unalloyed encomium upon "ancient" teachings. His approval of the ancients is actually restricted to one aspect of their life, and by

[12] Cf. IV, page 20. (WK transl.)

no means does it extend to all of their teachings. Rousseau rather ingeniously contrives in the *Poland* to present a myth of the ancients that excludes what one might well consider the most important feature of classical culture, its absorption with the questions of philosophy, and chooses instead to identify ancient virtue with the kind of political life created for Sparta by its founder, Lycurgus. One might indeed be justified in accusing Rousseau of having rejected the best and espoused the worst in his carefully biased portrayal of the ancients.

In any case, it is curious that Rousseau's version of ancient virtue is entirely compatible with the notion of "republican virtue" taught by that most notorious of "moderns," Niccolo Machiavelli.[13] Rousseau follows Machiavelli in his equation of the virtuous life with service to the state (or, to be more precise, he follows one part of Machiavelli's teaching, for the idea of republican virtue is not, I suspect, Machiavelli's final word concerning virtue), and he follows his predecessor in his attempt to undermine the authority of religion and classical political philosophy. In reading the *Poland* one should bear in mind Rousseau's peculiarly "modern" notion of "ancient" modes and orders: indeed the implications of Rousseau's selectivity with regard to the old leads one to question the seriousness of his repeated exhortations to return to ancient political forms. The regime proposed for the Poles and, by implication at least, for all other modern peoples is perhaps more radically new than the surface rhetoric of the *Poland* would lead us to suspect.

Thus far I have attempted to indicate the general outline of the peculiar ethos that Rousseau feels is a necessary prerequisite for effective legislation. The first task of the founder of a political regime for a modern people is to refashion the attitudes of his potential citizenry; only after this task has been successfully completed can one hope that the laws will be obeyed. Rousseau realizes, however, that to establish a favorable *ethos* is not by itself a sufficient solution to the problem of

[13] Cf. Leo Strauss' *Thoughts on Machiavelli* (Glencoe, Illinois: The Free Press, 1958).

refounding the modern state. He is still faced with the question of the large state with its attendant evils of despotism and inefficiency. Poland may be blessed with men whose souls approximate the grandeur of the souls of the ancients, but it is still an extensive territory with a large population concerning which Rousseau laments, "Large populations, vast territories: There you have the first and foremost reason for the misfortunes of mankind, above all the countless calamities that weaken and destroy polite peoples." [14] The problem now becomes that of securing the freedom of a small republic within the constitution of a large elective kingdom, and the dominant theme of the *Poland* changes from the philosophical treatment of Ancients and Moderns to the more practical analysis of the conditions necessary for representative government.

Rousseau's remedy for the evils that attend the large nation-state is the federal system. He envisages an association of numerous semiautonomous states bound together by a common legislature whose laws will be binding on each member but whose deliberation will be controlled by the individual constituent petty states. The representatives who deliberate at this grand assembly will be tied to mandates that have issued from prior deliberations at the level of the local assemblies. Rousseau seeks to avoid the kind of deliberative body whose members are concerned primarily with the interests of the large aggregate, in favor of a body composed of men who are devoted to the good of their particular communities. It must be admitted that Rousseau is not as clear as he could be on the question of the limits on the power of the central government. There is, for example, no list of prohibitions against the central authority in favor of the individual constituent states, as there is in the American Constitution. Furthermore, on the crucial issues of education and the administration of the extensive civil service system Rousseau is silent, so that it is difficult for us to determine whether he wants these areas to be under the exclusive control of the central government or under the direct management of the local dietines. However, Rousseau's pro-

[14] V, page 25. (WK transl.)

posal that the *liberum veto* be retained, though in a modified form,[15] in the new system indicates his concern for the rights of the localities over against the central power. Possessing this resource, any one of the individual dietines may check legislation on constitutional or other "fundamental" issues (Rousseau leaves it to the Poles to decide which laws other than constitutional amendments are in fact "fundamental") and thus protect its essential sovereignty against encroachments by the central government. Apparently, Rousseau feels that the combined forces of the two provisions—for instructed representatives and for the limited use of the *liberum veto*—will be sufficient to insure that degree of local autonomy which is his remedy for the evils of the large nation-state. The efficacy of such measures may be questioned, but it is clear enough that Rousseau wants to achieve the maximum degree of freedom within the federal system that will be consistent with the prior need of achieving Polish independence *vis-a-vis* the other European nations.

It is interesting to compare Rousseau's elaboration of his federal regime with the version of federalism proposed some twenty years later in America by Madison and Hamilton. The central problem of *The Federalist* is in essence the same problem that confronts Rousseau in the *Poland:* how to make possible the large republic that will avoid the despotic excesses of the large nation-states. But the different solutions offered by the two works are almost antithetical. Publius, on the one hand, develops a system that presupposes a high degree of diversity among the people of America. In fact he realizes that it is essential to foster diverse interests among the people since the interplay of these conflicting pursuits will safeguard

[15] Rousseau would have the Poles establish a board of review, which would consider particular uses of the veto and which would reward profusely those who used the veto justly while punishing severely, even with death, those who upon review were shown to have misused the privilege. He would also have the use of the veto restricted to certain "fundamental" laws. Cf. IX, pages 57–59. (WK transl.)

against the rise of tyrannous factional majorities. Secondly, Publius' legislative model works through the deliberations of representatives who are not previously instructed by their constituencies. *The Federalist* conceives of the legislative process as a kind of replay of the conflict between diverse interests that goes on in American society. The individual representatives are presumed to embody in some fashion the attitudes of the sections from which they are drawn, but they are not obligated by any specific mandate from their constituents. Finally, the federal system envisaged by Publius creates a central government that is so strong that it is indeed questionable whether in any meaningful sense the model can be called federal at all. *The Federalist* promises extensive freedoms to individuals under its proposed regime, but it is difficult to see how the work redeems its title by allowing any such equivalent liberties to the participating states. The central government counts for everything in the Madison-Hamilton model while the local communities count for nothing, or next to nothing.

Rousseau, by contrast, founds his political regime on a people who have been made more or less homogeneous through the inculcation of a national *ethos*. There is no room in his model for the competition of different social, economic and religious groups, which is the mainspring of the Publian model. Of course there must be expected a mutual striving for ascendancy among the men who seek to advance through the ranks of the civil service, but this is a carefully directed sort of competition, which benefits the whole polity while it smothers those radically divisive purposes fostered by selfishness or by devotion to transcendent truths. Like Publius, Rousseau invests the supreme authority of his republic in the legislative branch (the elected king is conceived to be little more than an errand boy for the Diet, and his powers are rather less extensive than those of the President in the Publian model), but the representatives who comprise the national assembly are bound by law to act according to the instructions that have been previously given to them by their local assemblies. Finally, and again in contrast to the philosophy of *The Federalist*, Rousseau's system is designed to give the local communities a strong hand against the power of the central government. He seems to feel that the only sure means of providing against the despotism of the large nation-state is to decentralize the deliberative process so that the general wills of the local assemblies may assert themselves, when the occasion demands, against the incursions of the national legislature. Rousseau's system, in other words, is heavily weighted in favor of corporate interests beneath the national level, while on the contrary the Publian model is designed to achieve legislation that can be applied to all individuals irrespective of their subsidiary corporate allegiances. Rousseau's regime seems the more genuinely federal of the two models since it allows for a high degree of autonomy among the local communities, whereas one suspects that the federalism of Publius is open to question.

The Government of Poland acquires a further dimension of importance when we read it in the context of democratic theory, since along with The Federalist it is possibly the first attempt by a political theorist of great standing to apply principles of democratic theory to a concrete political regime. Thus the Poland not only gives us a new perspective, as I have tried to show, on some of the more puzzling features of Rousseau's earlier political thought; it also provides us with a model for representative government which, because it is in many ways opposed to the prevailing Publian version, enables us to better understand both the virtues and the limitations of our current practices. To return to the promise implicit in the title of this Introduction, The Government of Poland should be read both as a clarification and a criticism of the political teaching of The Social Contract and as a comprehensive attempt to deal with those central problems of democratic theory that have continued to exercise our minds to this day.

Willmoore Kendall

University of Dallas
(August, 1966)

I

THE ISSUE POSED

Anyone who proposes to work out a master plan for reforming the government of Poland can learn much from the outline
prepared by Count Wielhorski, and from the accompanying
commentary as well.

I know of no one better qualified to elaborate such a plan
than Count Wielhorski. He possesses, over and above the general knowledge that the task demands, a knowledge of the lo-
cale, of the specific details which, though they can never be set
down in writing, must be taken into account by anyone seeking to fit legislation to the people for whom it is intended. One
must know thoroughly the nation for which one is building;
otherwise the final product, however excellent it may be in itself, will prove imperfect when it is acted upon—the more
certainly if the nation be already formed, with its tastes, customs, prejudices, and failings too deeply rooted to be stifled by
new plantings. Only the Poles themselves, or someone who has
made a thorough first-hand study of the Polish nation and its
neighbors, can devise good legislation for Poland. An outsider
can hardly contribute more than general observations, intended not to guide your institution-builder but to cast some
light on his problem. Even when my mind was at its best, I

1

could not have grasped all the broad relationships involved. Now, when I am barely able to tie one idea to another, I must confine myself—if I am to obey Count Wielhorski and give earnest of my zeal for his country—to reporting to him certain impressions I have received in the course of reading his work, and some reflections that it has suggested to me.

As one reads the history of the government of Poland, it is hard to understand how a state so oddly constituted can have survived for so long. I see a body of great size: many of its members are already dead, and the remainder have no unity, so that their motions, well-nigh independent of each other, far from serving any common end, cancel one another out. It labors mightily without accomplishing anything; it is unable to offer the slightest resistance to anyone who seeks to impose his will upon it; it falls apart five or six times in each century; it is paralyzed the moment it tries to put forth any effort or to provide for one of its needs; and, despite all these things, it nevertheless lives and keeps itself strong. There, to my mind, you have one of the strangest spectacles that ever forced itself upon the attention of a thinking man. I see all the states of Europe hastening to their doom. Monarchies and republics alike, nations that started out with the most magnificent legislation, fine, wisely-balanced systems of government—all are threatened with early death. But Poland, depopulated, devastated, and oppressed, wide-open to its aggressors, in the depths of misfortune and of anarchy, still shows all the fire of youth. It makes bold, as if it had just sprung to life, to demand government and laws! Poland is in irons but is busy discussing means of remaining free and feels within itself the kind of strength no tyranny is strong enough to conquer. I am reminded of the beleaguered Romans, tranquilly disposing of title to the very land upon which the enemy has just pitched camp.

Think twice, brave Poles! Think twice, lest by seeking to be too well off you make yourselves less well off than you are now. Never forget, as you dream of what you wish to gain, what you might lose. Correct the abuses of your constitution if you can; but do not think poorly of it. It has made you what you are.

You prize your freedom, and have deserved it. You have defended it against a powerful and wily aggressor who falsely offered you ties of friendship at the very time when he was fastening the irons of servitude upon your limbs. Today, exhausted by your country's trials, you sigh for peace. Peace seems to me easy to come by; what is difficult, to my way of thinking, is to keep it, and liberty along with it. You find anarchy hateful; but it was anarchy that formed in its bosom the hearts of those patriots who saved you from the yoke. Time was when they were falling deeply into lethargic slumber; the storm awakened them. Now, having smashed the irons that were forged for them, they stagger under the burden of their fatigue. They would like to combine the sweets of freedom with the peace and quiet that accompany despotism. They wish, I believe, for two things that cannot keep house together. Peace, in my opinion, is incompatible with freedom. One must choose.

This is not to say that things must be left as they are; but it is to say that you must lay hands on them only with extreme caution. At this moment you are more conscious of your ills than of your blessings. The time will come, I fear, when you will value the blessings more highly; and that, alas, will be when you have lost them.

It is an easy matter to make better laws? So be it. What is impossible is to make laws that the passions of men will not corrupt—just as they had corrupted the laws previously in effect; and to foresee and evaluate all the forms this corruption will take is, perhaps, beyond the powers of even the most consummate statesman. Putting law over men is a problem in politics that I like to compare to that of squaring the circle in geometry. Solve that problem correctly, and the government based upon your solution will be a good government, proof against corruption. But until you solve it, rest assured of this: you may think you have made the laws govern; but men will do the governing.

A good and sound constitution is one under which the law holds sway over the hearts of the citizens; for, short of the moment when the power of legislation shall have accomplished precisely that, the laws will continue to be evaded. But how to reach men's hearts? Our present-day lawgivers, thinking exclusively in terms of coercion and punishment, pay almost no attention to that problem—for which, perhaps, material rewards are no better solution. And justice, even the purest justice, is not a solution either. For justice, like good health, is a blessing that people enjoy without being aware of it, that inspires no enthusiasm, and that men learn to value only after they have lost it.

By what means, then, are we to move men's hearts and bring them to love their fatherland and its laws? Dare I say? Through the games they play as children, through institutions that, though a superficial man would deem them pointless, develop habits that abide and attachments that nothing can dissolve.

If in saying all this I am out of my wits, at least I am completely out of them. For I confess that I see in my folly all the hall-marks of reasonableness.

II

THE SPIRIT
OF ANCIENT
INSTITUTIONS

As we read the history of the ancients, it seems to us that we have moved into another universe and are surrounded by beings of another species. Our Frenchmen, our Englishmen, our Russians—what have they in common with the Romans and the Greeks? Almost nothing except the shape of their bodies. The Romans and Greeks, with their hardy spirits, seem to the man of our day a tall tale invented by the historians. How can he, who feels so puny, imagine that such great men ever actually existed? But they did exist; and they were human, just as we are.

What prevents us from being the kind of men they were? The prejudices, the base philosophy, and the passions of narrow self-interest which, along with indifference to the welfare of others, have been inculcated in all our hearts by ill-devised institutions, in which we find no trace of the hand of genius.

I gaze out over the nations of the modern world, and I see numerous scribblers of laws, but not a single legislator. But among the ancients I find no less than three legislators so outstanding as to deserve our special mention: Moses, Lycurgus, and Numa, all of whom concerned themselves mainly with matters that our doctors of learning would deem absurd. Yet each of them achieved a kind of success which, were it not so thoroughly supported by evidence, we should regard as impossible.

The first of the three conceived and executed this astonishing feat: he founded the body of a nation, using for his materials a swarm of wretched fugitives who possessed no skills, no arms, no talents, no virtues, and no courage, and who, without an inch of territory to call their own, were truly a troop of outcasts upon the face of the earth. Moses made bold to transform this herd of servile emigrants into a political society, a free people; at a moment when it was still wandering about in the wilderness and had not so much as a stone to pillow its head on, he bestowed upon it the enduring legislation—proof against time, fortune, and conquest—that five thousand years have not sufficed to destroy or even weaken. Even today, when that nation no longer exists as a body, its legislation endures and is as strong as ever.

Determined that his people should never be absorbed by other peoples, Moses devised for them customs and practices that could not be blended into those of other nations and weighted them down with rites and peculiar ceremonies. He put countless prohibitions upon them, all calculated to keep them constantly on their toes, and to make them, with respect to the rest of mankind, outsiders forever. Each fraternal bond that he established among the individual members of his republic became a further barrier, separating them from their neighbors and keeping them from becoming one with those neighbors. That is why this odd nation—so often subjugated, so often dispersed, so often, to all appearances, annihilated, but always utterly faithful to its law—has, scattered among other peoples but not absorbed by them, nevertheless preserved itself down into our own times. And that is why its customs, its laws, and its rites, live on—and, despite the hatred and persecution directed against it by all other men, will live on and on until the end of the world itself.

As for Lycurgus, he undertook to legislate for a people already debased by servitude and by the vices the latter brings in its train. He fixed upon them a yoke of iron, the like of which no other people has ever borne; but he tied them to that yoke, made them, so to speak, one with it, by filling up every moment of their lives. He saw to it that the image of the fatherland was constantly before their eyes—in their laws, in their games, in their homes, in their mating, in their feasts. He saw to it that they never had an instant of free time that they could call their own. And out of this ceaseless constraint, made noble by the purpose it served, was born that burning love of country which was always the strongest—or rather the only—passion of the Spartans, and which transformed them into beings more than merely human. Sparta, to be sure, was only a city; but the sheer force of its legislation made it lawgiver and capital to all of Greece and caused the Persian empire to tremble. With Sparta as a base, Spartan legislation extended its influence on all sides.

We come now to Numa. Those who regard this great man as merely an innovator of rites and religious ceremonies sorely misjudge him. Numa was the real founder of Rome. Romulus merely brought together a band of robbers that a single reverse could have broken up;[1] had it been left at that, Rome would have been a poor thing, unable to stand the test of time. It was Numa who bound Romulus' robbers together into an indissoluble body, and so gave Rome strength and permanence. He did this by transforming the robbers into citizens, not so much by means of laws, however—of laws they had, in their rustic poverty, scant need—as by mildly restrictive institutions that bound each of them to the rest and all of them to the soil; and, finally, by making their city sacred in their eyes by means of those rites, apparently idle and superstitious, whose strength and influence so few people have understood—although Romulus, fierce Romulus himself, had laid the foundations for them.

[1] [A free translation: the sentence, as Rousseau wrote it, reads: "If Romulus had done no more, etc.," thus suggesting that it was Romulus, not Numa, who did something more—which is, clearly, the opposite of the point intended.]

All notes in brackets are those of the translator.

All these legislators of ancient times based their legislation on the same ideas. All three sought ties that would bind the citizens to the fatherland and to one another. All three found what they were looking for in distinctive usages, in religious ceremonies that invariably were in essence exclusive and national,[2] in games that brought the citizens together frequently, in exercises that caused them to grow in vigor and strength and developed their pride and self esteem; and in public spectacles that, by keeping them reminded of their forefathers' deeds and hardships and virtues and triumphs, stirred their hearts, set them on fire with the spirit of emulation, and tied them tightly to the fatherland—that fatherland on whose behalf they were kept constantly busy. The oral recitations of the poetry of Homer, with the Greeks solemnly assembled as the body of the nation, in the open air, not cash-in-hand or in the midst of stalls and stages; the tragedies of Aeschylus, Sophocles, and Euripides, enacted over and over again with all Greece looking on; the prizes with which successful contestants in Greek games were crowned amidst applause from all their fellow-citizens—these are the things that, by constantly re-kindling the spirit of emulation and the love of glory, raised Greek courage and Greek virtues to a level of strenuousness of which nothing existing today can give us even a remote idea—which, indeed, strikes modern men as beyond belief. If these moderns have laws, it is only because they must be taught to obey smartly when their masters command them, to refrain from picking people's pockets, and to hand over large amounts of money to brazen scoundrels. If they have customs, it is only because they must learn to brighten the idle hours of courtesans and to promenade their mistresses in a graceful manner. If they assemble, it is in churches, for the sake of a cult which is in no sense national, which never in any way reminds them of their fatherland. Or if not in churches then in airless halls, in settings that are unmanly and dissolute, where they pay to listen to plays that are full of talk about nothing

[2] See the closing paragraphs of the *Social Contract* (IV, viii).

but love, of histrionic ranting, and of simpering by prostitutes—all in order to take lessons in corruption, these being, of all the lessons people claim to teach in plays, the only ones that yield financial returns. Or if not in theaters, then in public celebrations in which people, despised as always, have no voice whatever, and in which public blame and public approbation therefore count for nothing; or in disorderly crowds, which they join in search of new clandestine relationships, or of the kinds of pleasures that are divisive, that most isolate people from one another, and that most deaden the spirit.

Is all that likely to produce patriots? Is it any wonder that two ways of life that differ so profoundly should yield different fruits, and that men should now see in themselves no trace of the vigor of spirit that impelled the ancients in all they did?

Forgive these digressions—to a remaining spark of fervor that you have yourselves fanned into flame. It is a pleasure to speak again of that one of the peoples of our day that makes me feel closest to the men of old.

III
THE FOREGOING
APPLIED
TO POLAND

Poland is a large state, surrounded by yet larger states whose military discipline and despotic forms of government give them great offensive power. In sharp contrast to them, Poland is weak from anarchy, so that, despite the bravery of its citizens, it must accept any outrages its neighbors choose to inflict upon it. It has no fortified places to prevent their incursions into its territory. It is underpopulated, and is therefore well-nigh incapable of defending itself. It has no proper economic system. It has few troops, or rather none at all. It lacks military discipline. It is disorganized. Its people do not obey. Constantly divided within, constantly threatened from without, it has in itself no stability whatever and is at the mercy of its neighbors' whims.

As matters now stand, I see only one means of giving Poland the stability it lacks, namely, to infuse into the entire nation, so to speak, the spirit of your confederates, and to establish the republic in the Poles' own hearts, so that it will live on in them despite anything your oppressors may do. Those hearts are, to my mind, the republic's only place of refuge: there force can neither destroy it nor even reach it. Of this you have just seen a proof that will be remembered forever; Poland was in Russian irons, but the Poles themselves remained free—a great object lesson, which teaches you how you can defy the power and ambition of your neighbors. You cannot possibly keep them from swallowing you; see to it, at least, that they shall not be able to digest you. Whatever you do, your enemies will crush you a hundred times before you have given Poland what it needs in order to be capable of resisting them. There is one rampart, however, that will always be readied for its defense, and that no army can possibly breach; and that is the virtue of its citizens, their patriotic zeal, in the distinctive cast that national institutions are capable of impressing upon their souls. See to it that every Pole is incapable of becoming a Russian, and I answer for it that Russia will never subjugate Poland.

I repeat: *national* institutions. That is what gives form to the genius, the character, the tastes, and the customs of a people; what causes it to be itself rather than some other people; what arouses in it that ardent love of fatherland that is founded upon habits of mind impossible to uproot; what makes unbearably tedious for its citizens every moment spent away from home—even when they find themselves surrounded by delights that are denied them in their own country. Remember the Spartan at the court of the Great King: they chided him when, sated with sensual pleasures, he hungered for the taste of black broth. "Ah!" he sighed to the satrap, "I know your pleasures; but you do not know ours!"

Say what you like, there is no such thing nowadays as Frenchmen, Germans, Spaniards, or even Englishmen—only Europeans. All have the same tastes, the same passions, the same customs, and for good reason: Not one of them has ever been formed *nationally*, by distinctive legislation. Put them in the same circumstances and, man for man, they will do exactly the same things. They will all tell you how unselfish they are, and act like scoundrels. They will all go on and on about the public good, and think only of themselves. They will all sing the praises of moderation, and each will wish himself a modern

Croesus. They all dream only of luxury, and know no passion except the passion for money; sure as they are that money will fetch them everything they fancy, they will all sell themselves to the first man who is willing to pay them. What do they care what master's bidding they do, or what country's laws they obey? Their fatherland is any country where there is money for them to steal and women for them to seduce.

Give a different bent to the passions of the Poles; in doing so, you will shape their minds and hearts in a national pattern that will set them apart from other peoples, that will keep them from being absorbed by other peoples, or finding contentment among them, or allying themselves with them. You will give the Poles a spiritual vigor that will end all this iniquitous bandying-about of idle precepts, and will cause them to do by inclination and passionate choice the things that men motivated by duty or interest never do quite well enough. Upon souls like that, a wisely-conceived legislation will take firm hold. They will obey, not elude, the laws, because the laws will suit them, and will enjoy the inward assent of their own wills. They will love their fatherland; they will serve it zealously and with all their hearts. Where love of fatherland prevails, even a bad legislation would produce good citizens. And nothing except good citizens will ever make the state powerful and prosperous.

I shall describe below a system of administration that, leaving the deeper levels of your laws virtually untouched, seems to me what you need in order to raise the patriotism of the Poles, as also the virtues that invariably accompany patriotism, to their highest possible level of intensity. But whether you adopt that system or not, you must still begin by giving the citizens of Poland a high opinion of themselves and of their fatherland. That opinion, in view of the manner in which they have just shown themselves, will not be unfounded, which is to say: Seize the opportunity afforded by the events of the present moment, and raise souls to the pitch of the souls of the ancients. The Confederation of Bar saved your fatherland at a moment when it was about to expire; so much is certain.

Now: the story of that glorious episode should be carved in sacred characters upon each Polish heart. I should like you to erect, to the Confederation's memory, a monument inscribed with the name of every one of its members, including, since so great a deed should wipe out the transgressions of an entire lifetime, even those who may subsequently have betrayed the common cause. I should also like you to establish the custom of celebrating the confederates' deeds every ten years in solemn ceremonies—with the pomp appropriate to a republic: simple and proud rather than ostentatious and vain; and in them, with dignity and in language free from exaggeration, let praise be bestowed upon the virtuous citizens who had the honor to suffer for their country in the toils of the enemy. And finally, I should like some honorific distinction, one that would constantly remind the public of this noble heritage from the past, to be conferred even upon the Confederates' families. During these solemnities I should not, however, like you to permit any invective against the Russians, or even any mention of them. That would be to honor them too much; besides which your silence about them at the very moment of remembering their cruelty, and your praise for the men who resisted them, will say about the Russians all that needs be said. You should despise them too much ever to hate them.

I should like you, by means of honors and public prizes, to shed luster on all the patriotic virtues, to keep the Poles' minds constantly on the fatherland, making it their central preoccupation, and to hold it up constantly before their eyes. This, I admit, would give them less opportunity and leave them less time for getting rich, but they would also have less desire and less need for riches: their hearts would come to know happiness of another kind than that which wealth confers. There you have the secret for ennobling men's souls and for making of their ennoblement an incentive more powerful than gold.

I have not been able, from the brief sketch of Polish customs that M. de Wielhorski has kindly placed in my hands, to form an adequate picture of the Poles' civil and domestic us-

ages. But so large a country, and one that has never had much
intercourse with its neighbors, must have developed a great
many usages that are its very own but are perhaps being bas-
tardized, day in and day out, in line with the Europe-wide
tendency to take on the tastes and customs of the French. You
must maintain or revive (as the case may be) your ancient customs and introduce suitable new ones that will also be purely
Polish. Let these new customs be neither here nor there as far
as good and bad are concerned; let them even have their bad
points; they would, unless bad in principle, still afford this advantage: they would endear Poland to its citizens and develop
in them an instinctive distaste for mingling with the peoples of
other countries. I deem it all to the good, for example, that the
Poles have a distinctive mode of dress; you must take care to
preserve this asset—by doing precisely what a certain czar,
whose praises we often hear, did not do. See to it that your
king, your senators, everyone in public life, never wear anything but distinctively Polish clothing, and that no Pole shall
dare to present himself at court dressed like a Frenchman.

I recommend numerous public games, where Poland, like
a good mother, can take delight in seeing her children at play.
Let Poland's mind be on them often, so that their minds will
always be on Poland. You should prohibit—even, because of
the example, at court—the amusements that one ordinarily
finds in courts: gambling, the theater, comedies, operas—
everything that makes men unmanly, or distracts them, or iso-
lates them, or causes them to forget their fatherland and their
duties, or disposes them to feel content anywhere so long as
they are being amused. You must create games, festivities, and
ceremonials, all peculiar to your court to such an extent that
one will encounter nothing like them in any other. Life in Poland must be more fun than life in any other country, but not
the same kind of fun. This is to say: you must turn a certain
execrable proverb upside-down, and bring each Pole to say
from the bottom of his heart: *Ubi patria, ibi bene.*

If possible, let none of the things I have mentioned be reserved for the rich and powerful. Rather let there be frequent

open-air spectacles in which different ranks would be carefully distinguished, but in which, as in ancient times, all the people would take equal part. There, on certain occasions, let your young nobles try their strength and skill. Look at Spain, where the bullfights have done much to keep a certain vigor alive in the people. For the same purpose, Poland should take care to revive the circuses in which its young men used to take their exercise, and make of them arenas of honor and competition. Nothing could be easier than to work out, instead of the fights for which the circuses were customarily used, competitions that would be less cruel in character, yet would call for strength and skill, with, as in the past, honors and prizes for the victors. Competitions in horsemanship, for example, would be well-suited to the Poles and would lend themselves to spectacular display.

Homer's heroes all distinguished themselves by feats of strength and skill, and by doing so proved in the very eyes of the people that they were born to command them. So too with the man—hardy and courageous, eager for honor and glory, disciplined in all the virtues—who bore the stamp of the knightly tournaments. Because of firearms, bodily strength and skill now play a much lesser role in warfare than they used to, and so have fallen into discredit. But the result is that the man who possesses the advantage of good birth can now point to nothing within himself that sets him apart from other men and justifies his good fortune, no mark inseparable from his person that attests to his natural right to superiority—except for the qualities of mind and spirit, which are often open to dispute, turn up often in the wrong place, often lend themselves to deceit, and are of such character that the people are poor judges of them. The more we neglect these external signs, moreover, the safer we make it for those who govern us to become unmanly and corrupt. It is important, far more so than people think, that those who are some day to exercise command over others should prove themselves, from early youth, superior to those others in every sense—or at least try to. More: it is a good thing for the people to be thrown with them frequently on occasions set aside for pleasure, to learn to recognize them, to become accustomed to seeing them, and to share their amusements with them. Provided only that distinctions of rank are maintained and that the people never actually mingle with the rulers, this is the way to tie the former to the latter with bonds of affection, and to combine attachment to them with respect. Finally, delight in physical exercise discourages the dangerous kind of idleness, unmanly pleasures, and luxury of spirit. It is for the soul's sake, above all, that one must exercise the body. But this is something our puny sages are still far from having learned.

By no means omit a certain amount of public display, but let it be noble and impressive, and let it express its magnificence through persons, not things. Far more than people believe, men's hearts follow their eyes and respond to ceremonial majesty; it surrounds authority with an aura of order and discipline that inspires confidence, and that draws a line between authority and those notions of capriciousness and improvisation that keep company with the idea of arbitrary power. Only avoid, in the adornment of your solemnities, the tinsel and glitter and sumptuous décor that are usually to be seen at court. A free people's celebrations should breathe good taste and gravity; nothing unworthy of its esteem should be held up to it for admiration. The Romans displayed great luxury in their triumphs? But that was the luxury of the vanquished, so that the more it shone the less it seduced; and its very brilliance pointed up a great lesson for the Roman people. There were chains of gold and precious stones, but it was captive kings who were weighted down with them. There you have luxury correctly understood! Often, moreover, there are two entirely different routes leading to the same destination. The two woolsacks in front of the Lord Chancellor in the English House of Lords, for example, seem to me a decorative touch that is both moving and inspired. And two sheaves of wheat similarly placed in the Polish Senate would, in my eyes, produce a similarly handsome effect.

There is a great obstacle to the reforms needed to make love of country the governing passion, namely, the great differences in wealth between your magnates and your lesser nobles. So long as luxury rules in the homes of the powerful, covetousness will rule in the hearts of all. That which is the object of public admiration is always the object of individual desire, and where a man must be rich in order to shine, the governing passion will be that of getting rich. Here, then, is a broad avenue to corruption that must be closed off as completely as possible. If there were other inducements, if distinctions of rank were associated with high public office, they would be beyond the reach of the man with nothing to point to but his wealth; for if all other paths were closed off, private desires would channel themselves naturally into the path leading to those honorable distinctions, namely, that of merit and virtue. The Roman consuls were often quite poor, but they had their lictors; men coveted the display connected with the lictors, and the day came when plebeians won their way up to the consulate.

It is, I concede, extremely difficult to root out luxury completely where inequality is the rule. But might it not be possible to change the form luxury takes, and so render its example less pernicious? In the past, for instance, the poorer Polish nobles attached themselves to this or that magnate, who paid for their education and provided subsistence for them in his retinue. That is luxury of a kind that is great and noble. I am fully aware of its disadvantages, but it does, at least, raise the level of men's souls instead of debasing them, and develops their feelings, and gives them vigor; in Rome, for instance, it produced no harmful results while the republic endured. I have read that the Duke of Epernon met up one day with the Duke of Sully, and would have liked to pick a quarrel with him. Since, however, Epernon had only six hundred gentlemen in his suite, against Sully's eight hundred, he did not dare to attack him. I question if luxury of that kind leaves much room for the luxury that decks itself out in trinkets, and certainly it sets no examples that will seduce the poor. See to it that Poland's great lords once again indulge no other kind of luxury; it may result in factions, parties, and quarrels, but it will not corrupt the nation.

Next in order, let us look with a tolerant eye on military display, which is a matter of weapons and horses. But let all kinds of womanish adornment be held in contempt. And if you cannot bring women themselves to renounce it, let them at least be taught to disapprove of it, and view it with disdain, in men.

One further point: one does not stamp out luxury with sumptuary laws. You must reach deep into men's hearts and uproot it by implanting there healthier and nobler tastes. Merely prohibiting the things people should not do is a clumsy expedient and a pointless one, unless you see to it first that those things are hated and despised; and the law's disapproval is never efficacious except as it reinforces disapproval on the part of the citizens' own judgment. He who would try his hand at founding a nation must learn to dominate men's opinions, and through them to govern their passions. Sumptuary laws, instead of extinguishing desire by punishing it, stimulate desire by attempting to constrain it. And simplicity, whether of conduct or of attire, is less the product of law than of education.

IV
EDUCATION

Here we have the important topic: it is education that you must count on to shape the souls of the citizens in a national pattern and so to direct their opinions, their likes, and dislikes that they shall be patriotic by inclination, passionately, of necessity.

The newly-born infant, upon first opening his eyes, must gaze upon the fatherland, and until his dying day should behold nothing else. Your true republican is a man who imbibed love of the fatherland, which is to say love of the laws and of liberty, with his mother's milk. That love makes up his entire existence: he has eyes only for the fatherland, lives only for his fatherland; the moment he is alone, he is a mere cipher; the moment he has no fatherland, he is no more; if not dead, he is worse-off than if he were dead.

Truly national education belongs exclusively to men who are free; they and they only enjoy a common existence; they and they only are genuinely bound together by laws. Your Frenchman, your Englishman, your Spaniard, your Italian, your Russian, are all pretty much the same man; and that man emerges from school already well-shaped for license, which is to say for servitude. When the Pole reaches the age of twenty, he must be a Pole, not some other kind of man. I should wish him to learn to read by reading literature written in his own country. I should wish him, at ten, to be familiar with everything Poland has produced; at twelve, to know all its provinces, all its roads, all its towns; at fifteen, to have mastered his country's entire history, and at sixteen, all its laws; let his mind and heart be full of every noble deed, every illustrious man, that ever was in Poland, so that he can tell you about them at a moment's notice. I do not, as that should make clear, favor putting the youngsters through the usual round of studies, directed by foreigners and priests. The content, the sequence, even the method of their studies should be specified by Polish law. They should have only Poles for teachers—all of them married men, if that were possible, all men of distinction, alike for their conduct, their probity, their good sense, and their lights, and all destined, after a certain number of years of creditable service as teachers, to fill not more important posts, for there is none more important, but more prestigious and less-exacting ones. Above all, do not make the mistake of turning teaching into a career. A public servant in Poland should have no permanent status other than that of citizen; each post he fills, especially if it be an important one like that of teacher, should be thought of merely as one further testing-ground, one further rung on a ladder, from which to climb, when he deserves to, yet higher. I urge the Poles to give heed to this principle, upon which I shall often insist; I believe it to be a key with which the state can unlock a great storehouse of energy. And the reader will see below how, in my opinion, it can be made workable in all cases.

I do not like at all those lines you draw between your schools and academies, with the result that your rich nobles are brought up differently, and in different institutions, from your poor ones. Since all of them are equal under Poland's constitution, they should be brought up together, and in the same way; and if completely free public schools are out of the question, you must at least make your schools cheap enough for the poor nobles to afford. Perhaps it would be possible to set aside a certain number of places in each of your schools for students who would pay no tuition at all, that is to say, places paid for by the state—as with what the French call "scholarships"? Such places could be conferred upon the children of poor gentlemen who had deserved well of the fatherland—not as charity but as proper payment for the valuable services of their fathers; they would come to be regarded, for that reason, as posts of honor, and might well produce two beneficial results that are not to be sneezed at. Appointments to them should not, therefore, be arbitrary, but rather should be made by a procedure that I shall explain below. The appointees would be called "wards of the fatherland," and they should be distinguished by some badge of honor that would give them precedence over other youngsters of their year, including even the children of the great lords.

Each school must have its gymnasium, where the youngsters will go to take physical exercise. This neglected side of education is, in my opinion, the most important of all, not only because it develops strong, healthy constitutions, but even more because of the moral objective of education, which people either slight or try to accomplish by means of a list of idle and pedantic precepts that are so much wasted breath. I cannot repeat too often that good education must always be negative education. Choke off vices before they are born, and you will have done on behalf of virtue all that needs doing; and, in a good public school system, the means of doing this are as easy as falling off of a log: you have merely to keep the children always on their toes—not with this or that tiresome classroom drill that they cannot understand and hate because it keeps them in a fixed spot, but with physical exercise, which they like because it satisfies the need of their growing bodies for activity, and for other reasons as well.

Do not let the students in your school go off by themselves to play, just for the fun of it. They should play together in public, and for some prize to which they all aspire and which arouses in them the spirit of competition and emulation.

Even parents who choose to have their children educated at home and brought up under their own eyes should be required to send them to these exercises. Let the instructions of their children go forward individually, and under the family roof; but let their games be public, and shared with all; for here it is not a question merely of keeping them busy, or of bringing them up with robust constitutions and agile, well-developed bodies, but also of getting them accustomed, from an early moment, to rules, to equality, to fraternity, to competitions, to living with the eyes of their fellow-citizens upon them, and to seeking public approbation. The prizes and rewards for the victorious contestants should, therefore, not be conferred arbitrarily, that is, by fiat of the coaches or the school heads, but by acclamation based on the verdict of the spectators. You can depend on it that the decisions will always be fair, especially if you take pains to make the games attractive to the public by organizing them with an eye to the ceremonial and the spectacular. If that be done, we may take it for granted that your good patriots and your honest folk will treat attendance as both a duty and a pleasure.

In Berne, they have a remarkable exercise that the young patricians go through when they leave school. They call it the "miniature state," and it reproduces, on a small scale, all the component parts of the government of the republic: the senate, the magistrates, the officials, the bailiffs, and the advocates; law-suits, decisions, ceremonies. The miniature state even has its own tiny territory and its own revenues; it draws its powers from, and is protected by, the sovereign, and so serves as an incubator for the statesmen who one day—performing functions that they first performed in a game—will administer the republic's affairs.

No matter what pattern you impose on your public education—for I am not concerned here with details—you will need a board of top-grade officials, with supreme authority, to administer it, and to appoint, remove, or transfer at will the principals and heads of the schools (who, as I have already indicated, will be candidates for the higher magistrature), and the teachers as well. As for the latter, care should be taken to stimulate their zeal and vigilance by promoting them or not promoting them to more responsible posts, depending on how they have performed their current tasks well or badly. The hope of the republic, the very glory and destiny of the nation, depend upon these institutions, which is why I attach to them—as I confess I do—an importance that others, to my astonishment, have nowhere dreamt of conceding them. My great regret for mankind is that so many ideas that I find to be good and useful, and highly practical on top of that, are still so far from being put into practice.

For the rest, I confine myself here to suggestions; nor do those to whom I address myself need anything more. The above remarks, inadequately developed though they are, point from afar to the paths—unknown to us moderns—along which the ancients led men up to that level of spiritual vigor, of patriotic zeal, of high esteem for the qualities that are truly personal and not foreign to the nature of man, of which we have no contemporary examples. Even now, however, the leaven they used is present in the hearts of all men, and awaits, in order to produce its fermentation, only activation by appropriate institutions. Point the education, the usages, the customs, the manners of the Poles in that direction, and you will activate that leaven, not yet gone flat from exposure to corrupt teachings, outmoded institutions, and a philosophy of egoism that preaches and kills. Your nation will date its second birth from the terrible crisis from which it is now emerging; seeing what its members once accomplished without benefit of discipline, it will expect much, and will obtain even more, from legislation that has been wisely meditated; it will cherish and respect its laws, which will do honor to its noble pride, which will make it happy and free and keep it happy and free; it will tear out of its bosom those passions that elude the laws, and nourish those that cause them to be loved; it will, in fine, renew itself through itself, and will take on again, in this new phase of its history, the vigor of a nation just being born. Without the precautions I have set forth, however, expect nothing from your laws; no matter how wise and far-seeing they may be, they will be got around and remain without effect. You will have corrected certain abuses that are now doing you hurt, but only to call into existence new ones, none of which you will have anticipated.

So much for certain preliminaries that I have deemed indispensable. Let us now turn our attention to your constitution.

V

THE RADICAL VICE

Let us, if possible, not start off by hurling ourselves into unrealistic proposals.

What, gentlemen, is the business you are about? Reforming the government of Poland, which is to say: giving to the constitution of a large kingdom the stability and vigor of that of a tiny republic. You should first ask yourselves, before laboring to accomplish that purpose, whether your efforts can possibly be successful.

Large populations, vast territories! There you have the first and foremost reason for the misfortunes of mankind, above all the countless calamities that weaken and destroy polite peoples. Almost all small states, republics and monarchies alike, prosper, simply because they are small, because all their citizens know each other and keep an eye on each other, and because their rulers can see for themselves the harm that is being done and the good that is theirs to do and can look on as their orders are being executed. Not so the large nations: they stagger under the weight of their own numbers, and their peoples lead a miserable existence—either, like yourselves, in conditions of anarchy, or under petty tyrants that the requirements of hierarchy oblige their kings to set over them. As God alone can govern the world, only men of more than human capacities would be able to govern a large nation. It is astonishing, miraculous even, that Poland's vast territorial extension has not already, on a hundred occasions, transformed its government into a despotism, debased the souls of its citizens, and corrupted the masses of its people; and for such a state, after many centuries, to have degenerated no further down than anarchy is a phenomenon without precedent in history; and if it has slipped downward thus slowly, it is only because of advantages that are inseparable from the evils from which you wish to deliver yourselves. I cannot possibly repeat it too often: think well before laying hands upon your laws, especially those that have made you what you are. The reform you ought to undertake first would be that of your territory; your vast provinces will never admit of the circumspect administration of the small republics. If you wish to reform your government, then, begin by narrowing your frontiers, though perhaps your neighbors intend to do that for you. It would certainly be a great misfortune for the dismembered parts, but a great blessing for the body of the nation.

If no such reduction takes place, I see only one measure that perhaps might do instead—happily, however, one that already falls within the spirit of your constitution. Let the line between the two Polands be as distinct as that between them and Lithuania; have three states united in one—indeed, if that were possible, I should wish you to have as many as you now have of palatinates. Create in each of these states as many regional administrations. Perfect the organization of your dietines, granting them wider powers within their respective palatinates. At the same time, however, fix the limits of those powers with great care, making sure that nothing can sever the bond of common laws, and of subordination to the main body of the republic, that ties them together. In a word, make it your business to extend and perfect the federal system of government, which is the only system that can meet your needs. If you ignore this recommendation, I question whether you will ever succeed in accomplishing a worthwhile reform.

VI

PROBLEM
OF THE THREE
ORDERS

I seldom hear anyone speak of government without noticing that the principles appealed to seem to me either false or disingenuous.

The republic of Poland, we are often told, is made up of three orders: the knightly order, the senate, and the king. I should say, rather, that the Polish *nation* [1] is made up of three orders: the nobles, who count for everything; the middle-class, who count for nothing; and the peasants, who count for less than nothing. If the senate is to be counted separately as an order within the state, why not—since it is no less distinct, and does not have less power—the chamber of deputies as well? Nor is that all: the division into three orders, even as currently understood, is incomplete on the face of it. It leaves out the ministers, who are neither kings nor senators nor deputies, but are, nevertheless, the depositaries of all executive power and as independent as they could possibly be. How is anyone going to explain to me that the part, which exists only in virtue of the whole, nevertheless constitutes, over against the whole, an independent order? I grant you England; there the peerage,

[1] [Italics added.]

27

since it is hereditary, does constitute an order with a separate existence. Not so in Poland; no one can be a senator who is not first a noble, so that if you take away the knightly order the senate ceases to exist. So also does the king; the knightly order elects him, and he can do nothing without its concurrence. But if you take away the senate and the king, the knightly order, and thereby the state and the sovereign as well, remain intact; and tomorrow, if the knightly order so wishes, there will be a senate and a king just as before.

The fact that the senate is not an order in the state does not, however, mean that it counts for nothing in the state. Even if it lost its status as the depositary of the laws, its individual members, independently of its authority as a body, would not be any the less depositaries of the legislative power; were they prevented from voting in any Diet plenum where laws were being passed or rescinded, that would be to deprive them of the right that belongs to them by birth—though they would, to be sure, vote then simply as citizens, not senators. The moment the legislative power speaks, all inequalities lapse; all other authorities are silent; its voice is the voice of God on earth. The king himself, I contend, though he presides over the Diet, has no right to cast a vote there unless he is a Polish noble.

Someone will undoubtedly object at this point that I am proving too much: if the senators cannot vote in the Diet as senators, they should not be able to as citizens either; the members of the knightly order do not vote individually in the Diet but only through their representatives; and the senators are not representatives. Which is to say: why should the senators vote in the Diet as individuals, when no other noble, unless he is a deputy, can do so? The point, as matters now stand, seems to me well taken, but it will cease to be that when the reforms projected here have been carried out, since each of the senators will then be, in his own right, the permanent representative of the nation, though unable to act on matters of legislation without the concurrence of his colleagues.

Let no one try to tell me, then, that the concurrence of

king, senate, and knightly order is necessary for making a law. The power to make laws belongs exclusively to the knightly order: the senators, like the deputies, are indeed members of that order, but the senate as a body has no place in it. Such is, or appears to be, the law of the Polish state. But the law of nature, sacred and imprescriptible, which addresses itself to man's heart and man's reason, does not permit us to confine the legislative authority within such narrow limits or to make the laws binding upon any person who has not cast his vote on them either in person, like the deputies, or at least through chosen representatives, like the nobles as a body. That sacred law is not to be violated with impunity; and the condition of weakness to which so great a nation as yours now finds itself reduced is the product of that feudal barbarism that cuts off from the body of the state its most numerous, and from some points of view its most wholesome, part.

God forbid that I should deem it necessary to offer proof here for something of which a little good sense and feeling will persuade any man. And from what source, I ask you, does Poland propose to recoup the might and energy she is wantonly smothering in her own bosom? Nobles of Poland, be more than nobles, be men; only when you are men will you be happy and free. But do not flatter yourselves that you are either so long as you keep your own brothers in bondage.

I am aware of the difficulties involved in the proposal that you enfranchise the masses of your people; and what I am afraid of is not merely the misguided self-interest, the pride, and the prejudices of the owners. Even with that obstacle out of the way, I should still be afraid of the vices and slavishness of the serfs themselves. Liberty is a food that is good to taste but hard to digest: it sets well only on a good strong stomach. I laugh at those debased peoples that let themselves be stirred up by agitators and dare to speak of liberty without so much as having the idea of it; with their hearts still heavy with the vices of slaves, they imagine that they have only to be mutinous in order to be free. Proud, sacred liberty! If they but knew her, those wretched men; if they but understood the price at which she is won and held; if they but realized that her laws are stern as the tyrant's yoke is never hard, their sickly souls, the slaves of passions that would have to be hauled out by the roots, would fear liberty a hundred times as much as they fear servitude. They would flee her in terror as they would a burden about to crush them.

The emancipation of the Polish serfs is a great and noble enterprise but daring and hazardous as well, so that it should not be undertaken lightly. Among the precautions you would be well-advised to take, one at least is indispensable and will take some time, namely, to start out by making the serfs you wish to emancipate worthy of liberty and capable of bearing it. I shall set forth below one of the methods by which that might be done. It would be over-daring for me to guarantee its success, for all that I have no doubts about it; besides which if there is some better method, let it be adopted. But keep yourselves reminded, whatever the method, of this: your serfs are men, even as you are; they have in them the capacity to become everything that you are; your first task is to set that capacity to work, and not to free their bodies before you have freed their souls. Without that preliminary step, depend on it that the enterprise will turn out badly.

VII

MEANS
OF MAINTAINING
THE CONSTITUTION

The laws of Poland, like all the laws of Europe, were made little by little, by bits and pieces: an abuse appeared, and a law was made to deal with it. That law gave rise to further abuses, and these had to be dealt with in the same manner. With that sort of thing there is no stopping-point, and it leads finally to the most terrible abuse of all, which is the weakening of all the laws by the adding of new ones.

Legislation was brought low in Poland in a way that is quite unusual and perhaps unique: it lost its vigor without being subjugated by the executive power. Even now your legislative power retains its full authority; it is inactive, but it has nothing above it. The Diet is no less sovereign than it was when it was established. But it has no power; nobody dominates it, but nobody obeys it. This is a remarkable state of affairs, which merits careful thought.

What did preserve your legislative power up to the present moment? The continual presence of the legislature. Frequent Diets, frequent renewal of mandates—these are the things that sustained your republic. England, which enjoys the first of these blessings, lost its freedom because it had neglected the second. One and the same parliament sits for so long that the court, which would run out of money if it had to buy parliament every year, can well afford to buy it for seven, and does not fail to do so. Lesson number one for you.

A second means by which the legislative power was preserved in Poland is, for one thing, the sharing out of executive power, which kept the latter's depositaries from acting in concert to oppress the legislature; and, for another, the frequent passing of the executive power from hand to hand, which prevented any sustained scheme of usurpation. Each of your kings, in the course of his reign, took steps in the direction of arbitrary power; but when his successor was elected, he was obliged to draw back rather than press forward. At the beginning of his reign each king had, because of the *pacta conventa*, to start out from the same point as all the others; so that despite the general drift toward despotism, your kings made no progress in that regard.

The same thing may be said of your ministers and your higher officials. All of them, independent both of the senate and of one another, exercised unlimited authority, each within his own department; but entirely apart from the fact that the offices balanced one another because they were not handed down in one and the same family, they themselves carried with them no absolute power: all power, even when it was usurped, always reverted to its original source. Things would have fallen out quite differently had all executive power been concentrated in a single body like the senate, or in a single family because of a hereditary crown. Soon or late that family or that body would probably have brought the legislative power to heel, and so would have fastened upon the Poles the same yoke that all nations today have upon their necks. The Poles alone have escaped it, since the time has passed when I could have mentioned the Swedes in this connection. Lesson number two for you.

So much for your blessings, which are undoubtedly great; but here is the disadvantage, hardly smaller, that they carry with them. Executive authority, when it is parcelled out among several individuals, lacks harmony and produces a continual tug-of-war that is incompatible with right order. Each depositary of a part of the executive power places himself, in virtue of that part, above the magistrates and the laws in every respect. Each, to be sure, recognizes the authority of the Diet; but, recognizing no other authority, each recognizes no authority whatever once the Diet is dissolved; each despises the tribunals and defies their rulings. They are so many minor despots: without precisely usurping sovereign authority, they nevertheless oppress the citizens in particular situations and set a vicious example, too often imitated, by ruthlessly and brazenly violating the rights and liberty of individuals.

There, I believe, you have the first and foremost cause of the anarchy that prevails in Poland. I see only one way to remove it. You will not do so by arming special tribunals with the public power to coerce these petty tyrants; such a power, now because of bad administration, now because it would run afoul of some greater force, might stir up the unrest and disorder that could grow, little by little, into civil wars. What is needed is to vest all executive power in a permanent and respected single body, like the senate, which would be able, because of its stability and authority, to confine within the bounds of their duty any magnates that might be tempted to exceed them. This seems to be an effective means for meeting the problem, and it certainly would meet it; but the attendant danger would be terrible, and extremely difficult to avoid. For, as is made clear in my *Social Contract*, every body that is the depositary of executive power has a strong and persistent tendency to subordinate the legislative power, and sooner or later succeeds in doing so.

The proposal has been made, by way of avoiding the above danger, that you split the senate up into several councils or departments, each presided over by the minister responsible for that department, and have each minister and councilmember move to a different assignment after a fixed interval of time, that is, change places with another minister or council-member. This idea—it comes from the Abbé de Saint

Pierre, who developed it at length in his *Polysynodie*—may be a good one. Executive power, thus parcelled out and passed constantly from hand to hand, will indeed be more under the control of the legislative power, and the several areas of specialization within the administrative process will indeed, thus separated, be better explored and more skillfully handled. You must not, however, count too much on such an arrangement. If departments are always held at arm's length from one another, they will lack concert; and soon, working at cross-purposes, they will be using nearly all their energies against one another—until, finally, one of them has won the ascendancy and dominates them all; or, if that does not happen, they may come to terms and act together, in which case they will become a single body with a single mind, like the chambers of a parliament. In either case, I contend, it will be impossible to maintain such independence and equilibrium among them as will prevent the formation, in the long run, of an administrative center, or focal point, where all particular powers will be pooled in order to oppress the sovereign. In almost all of our republics, the councils are split up in this way among several departments that were independent of one another to begin with but soon ceased to be.

This whole business of drawing of lines—between chambers, between departments—is a modern invention. The ancients, who knew much more than we know about the preserving of freedom, were ignorant of any such expedient. Rome's senate governed half the known world, but the idea of dividing itself into parts never so much as crossed its mind. Yet it never succeeded in oppressing the legislative power, for all that its members had life tenure. But Rome's laws had censors, and the Roman people had tribunes; and the senate did not elect the consuls.

The way to get good, vigorous, effective administration is to concentrate all executive power in the same hands; but, having done that, merely changing the hands is not enough. The hands must, if possible, act only under the eyes of the legislature, and with its guidance. That is the real secret for seeing to it that they do not usurp legislative power.

So long as your estates continue to assemble and your deputies continue to be frequently replaced, it will be difficult for your senate or your king to encroach upon or usurp the legislative power. I deem it remarkable that your kings, up to now, have never attempted to lengthen the interval between Diets, and this despite the fact that, unlike the kings of England, they have not been obliged to convoke them frequently on pain of running out of money. Either a) your affairs must always have been in a state of crisis that has kept your kings from getting power enough to take the necessary steps, or b) your kings must have made sure, by means of intrigues in the dietines, of having a majority of the deputies always at their disposal, or c) your kings, because of the *liberum veto*, must always have been sure that they could arrest any legislative proceeding that might displease them, and dissolve the Diet at their pleasure. You can take it for granted, however, that once all these conditions no longer obtain, the king, or the senate, or the two together, will go to great lengths to free themselves from the Diets, and make them as infrequent as possible. That, above all, is what you must look forward to and forestall; and the method I have proposed is the only one that will work. It is simple; it cannot fail to produce the desired result; and it is odd that nobody had ever thought of it before the *Social Contract*,[1] in which I expound it.

One of the greatest drawbacks of large states, that which more than any other makes the preservation of liberty most difficult for them, is that the legislative power in such a state cannot make itself seen and can act only by deputation. This, to be sure, has its advantages as well as its disadvantages; but the latter outweigh the former. The legislator as a body is impossible to corrupt but easy to put upon. Its representatives are difficult to put upon but easy to corrupt; and it rarely happens that they are not corrupted. You have merely to look at the English parliament as one example, and at your own nation, because of the *liberum veto*, as another. Now: one can enlighten the man who is mistaken, but how restrain the man who can be bought? Without being an expert on Polish affairs I should

[1] III, xiii.

bet anything that your Diet is the place to look for enlightenment, and your dietines the place to look for virtue.

I see two means of preventing the shocking evil of corruption, which transforms the organ of liberty into that of servitude.

The first, as I have already said, is that of frequent Diets: by changing your deputies often, you will make them more costly and difficult to seduce. In this regard, your constitution is superior to Great Britain's; and once you have eliminated or modified the *liberum veto*, no further reform seems to me to be needed, unless to make more difficult the return of the same deputies to two consecutive Diets and so make sure that no single individual shall be elected repeatedly. I shall say more about this below.

The second means is that of tying the deputies to the letter of their instructions and to a strict accounting to their constituents for their conduct in the Diet. On this point, I can only record my astonishment at the irresponsibility and lack of caution, the stupidity even, of the English: having lodged supreme power in the hands of their deputies, they place no limitation on the use these deputies will be able to make of their power through the seven long years of their mandate.

The Poles are not, I think, sufficiently aware of the importance of the dietines; all that they owe to them already, all that they can accomplish with them in future by increasing their powers and by regularizing them somewhat. For I am convinced of this: if the confederations saved the fatherland from destruction in the past, it is the dietines that preserved its character. They are the true palladium of your freedom.

The dietines should draft the instructions to their deputies with great care, with an eye both to the topics listed in the convocation and to the current needs of the state or the province. The drafting committee for this purpose might, if you wished, have as its chairman the marshal of the dietine. But its remaining members should be elected by majority vote, and the members of the dietine should not go home until the instructions have been read, discussed, and approved in a plenary session. Besides the original copy of the instructions, which would be handed to the deputies along with their credentials, there should be a duplicate, which they would sign, to be held in the dietine's archives; it is with these instructions in hand that, upon their return, they should account for their actions in the Diet to the report-session of the dietine, which you absolutely must reestablish; and it is on the basis of this accounting that they should either a) be excluded from any subsequent mandate, or b), if they have carried out the instructions to the satisfaction of their constituents, be declared eligible for reelection. This audit is of the first importance; you could not possibly give it more attention than it deserves, or take too many pains to make its meaning clear to everybody. The deputy, every time he opens his mouth in the Diet, every time he takes any action there of any kind, must see himself on the carpet before his constituents and keep himself reminded that their judgment upon him will influence both his plans for advancement and the good reputation that he must have among his compatriots in order to carry them out. In a word, the nation does not send deputies to the Diet to give voice to their own sentiments but to declare the nation's own will; and such a brake as I have described is absolutely necessary, both for holding them to their duties and for preventing corruption, of whatever kind and from whatever source. Say what you like, I see no objection to limiting the deputies in this way, especially as the Chamber of Deputies has, or should have, nothing to do with administrative details, and therefore cannot be called upon to deal with any unforeseen topic. For the rest, a deputy's constituents, provided he has done nothing contrary to their expressed wishes, are not going to deem it a crime if, speaking merely as a good citizen, on some unforeseen topic concerning which they have made no decision, he has expressed an opinion. Let me add, finally, even if holding the deputies thus strictly to their instructions did have some disadvantages, these would still be a small matter over against the immense benefit of a law that would never fail to be the faithful expression of the nation's will.

Once the above precautions have been taken, however, there must never be any jurisdictional conflict between the Diet and the dietines. I do not concede, even to the dietines, any right to protest a law that has been sanctioned by the Diet plenum. Let the dietines, by all means, punish their deputies; let them, if need arises, have their deputies' heads cut off for betraying their confidence, but let the dietines, at the same time, obey—to the letter, always, without exception, and without protests. Which is to say: let them, as it is only right they should, live with the consequences of their own bad choices—though without prejudice to their making representations, as vigorous as ever they like, in the next Diet.

If the Diets are frequent, there is less need for them to be long of life. Six weeks, I should say, should suffice for transacting the routine business of the state, but with this reservation: it is a contradiction in terms to say that the sovereign authority can put fetters on itself, especially when the nation holds it right in its own hands. Let the duration of the regular sessions of the Diet remain fixed at six weeks, then. No objection on my part. But there will still be nothing to keep it from prolonging its life beyond that term, when business makes it necessary, by passing a resolution to that effect. In a word: the Diet, in its very nature, is above the law; and if it says "*I wish to stay where I am*," who is to say to it "*I do not wish you to stay there*"? There is only one situation in which the Diet could not pass such a resolution, namely, where it attempted to prolong its life beyond two years; at the end of two years its powers expire, and those of the new Diet come into being. The Diet, since it can do anything it sees fit to do, can, indisputably, provide for a longer interval between Diets. But a new law to that effect would apply only to subsequent Diets, and the Diet that sanctioned it could not possibly benefit from it. I have demonstrated the principles from which these rules derive in my *Social Contract*.

A word now about special sessions: These, practically speaking, should be infrequent for the sake of good order. They should be called only in situations of urgent necessity.

The king, I grant, should be taken at his word when he declares that such a situation exists. But if an emergency exists, as it will sometimes, and the king does not recognize it, should the senate then be the judge? In a free state one must think forward to everything that might jeopardize freedom. The confederations, if they are retained, will in certain cases serve instead of special sessions of the Diet. But if you are to abolish the confederations, you will need, as a matter of course, legal provision for special sessions.

The laws cannot, in my opinion, reasonably put limits on the duration of special sessions; that must depend entirely upon the nature of the business for which they have been convoked. Usually, that business will require swift handling; but swiftness here is relative to the problems to be dealt with, which, since they are by definition not routine in character, cannot be provided for beforehand; you might find yourselves in a situation that would require the Diet to sit either until that situation changed, or until the date for a new Diet caused its powers to lapse.

The Diet's time being so precious, you should try to economize it by eliminating those idle debates that only eat time up. The Diet needs, to be sure, ritual and majesty as well as rules and good order, and I should like you to give particular attention to that item: for example, to the barbarousness, the shocking indecency, of letting the sanctuary of the laws be profaned by the brandishing of weapons. Poles, are you more warlike than the Romans? Never, even in the darkest days of the republic, were the Roman comitia and the Roman senate defiled by the sight of an unsheathed sword. Also, I should like the Diet to concentrate on what is important and necessary, and so avoid everything that can be done equally well elsewhere. The *rugi*, for instance, that is, the Diet's review of the deputies' credentials, is a sheer waste of the Diet's time—not because the review itself is unimportant, but because it can be done as well and better in the localities from which the deputies have been elected, where they are known better than elsewhere, and where they can face their challengers. There, in their own palatinate, in the dietines that have elected them, is the best place, and the quickest one, for determining the validity of their mandates—as you do already with those of the commissioners of Radom and the deputies to the Tribunal. Once the dietines have spoken, the Diet should seat the deputies without further discussion, on the basis of the credentials they present, so as to avoid both the obstacles that might delay the choice of a marshal, and, above all, the intrigues by which the senate or the king might trouble the elections and cheat persons not to their liking. What happened recently in London should be a lesson for the Poles. I do not have to be told that Wilkes is a mere mischief-maker, but the precedent established by unseating him sets the stage: henceforth only those who are acceptable to the court will gain admission to the House of Commons.

You must give more attention, first of all, to the procedure by which nobles become voting-members of the dietines. That would make it easier to determine eligibility for the Diet, and the Venetian "Book of Gold" is an example which, because of its convenience, you might well follow. Nothing could be simpler than for each *grod* to keep its own accurate roster of the nobles who meet all the qualifications for attending, and casting votes in, the dietine. They would be inscribed in the local register as they reached the age specified by the laws—and would be struck off, the grounds for striking them off having been duly entered, if and when they got themselves into a situation that called for excluding them. These rosters, kept in such fashion that no one could question their accuracy, would enable you to tell at a glance both the lawful members of the dietines, and the persons eligible to be deputies. The time devoted to debate on such questions would be greatly reduced.

Improved procedure, both in the Diet and in the dietines, would be a good idea; though I cannot repeat too often that you must not try to move in different directions at one and the same time. Order is good, but liberty is better; the more you tie liberty down with formal rules, the more the rules will open up avenues to usurpation; the rules you lay down to prevent license in legislative procedure, good though they be in and of themselves, will sooner or later be used to oppress the legislature. Long and idle harangues, which waste time where time is so precious, are indeed a great evil; but it is a still greater evil for a good citizen to be afraid to speak when he has useful things to say. If the moment ever comes when only such and such persons open their mouths in the Diet, and even they dare not say anything they like, Diet speeches will soon consist exclusively of what the powerful wish to hear.

After you have made the indispensable changes with respect to the appointment of officials and the distribution of honors, there will probably be fewer idle harangues, and fewer flattering speeches meant for the ears of the king. However, you would have less high-sounding oratory, fewer speeches that never come to the point, if you obliged each speaker, upon taking the floor, to state clearly the proposal he wishes to offer, and required him, once he set forth his arguments, to present his conclusions in summary form, as the king's attorneys do in the courts. Even if that did not give you shorter speeches, it would at least hold in check the deputies who like to talk on and on to kill time without saying anything.

I am not fully informed about the Diet's established practice in the matter of sanctioning laws. But I feel sure—for reasons that I have already set forth—that your rules on this point should not be those that govern the British Parliament. The Polish senate should be vested with administrative, not legislative, power; the senators should vote on legislative issues as members of the Diet, not as senators; and votes should be taken in the same way in both chambers, *i.e.*, by counting heads. Perhaps, up to now, the *liberum veto* has made it impossible to make such a distinction; [2] but with the *liberum veto* out of the way, it will be urgently needed—all the more because its abolition will be, in the Chamber of Deputies at least,

[2] [Apparently the distinction between the senators as senators and the senators as members of the Diet. The French is by no means clear.]

an immense advantage; for I assume that the senators, and even more certainly the ministers, have never had the veto privilege. The veto of the Polish deputies corresponds to that of the tribunes of the people in Rome, and they exercised it not as citizens but as representatives of the people. We can, then, speak of the "loss" of the *liberum veto* only in the Chamber of Deputies. The senate as a body loses nothing, and so comes out ahead.[3]

With that in mind, I see a defect in your Diet that needs to be remedied, namely, since there are almost as many senators as deputies, the senate has too great an impact on legislative decisions and, given the high regard in which it is held by the knightly order, can easily attract the small number of votes it needs in order to have its way about any and all matters. I call this a defect for the following reason: the senate, since it is a sectional body within the state, necessarily has sectional interests different from, and potentially contrary to, those of the nation. Now: the law, which is merely the expression of the general will, is certainly the product of the interplay of all sectional interests, combining with and balancing one another in all their variety. But the interests of corporate bodies, if given excessive weight, would upset the balance. They should, therefore, not be represented as such. Each individual should be heard, but corporate bodies should not be. If the senate were over-represented in the Diet, it would not only carry its interest with it into the sessions, but would cause that interest to prevail.

One natural remedy for this defect leaps to the mind, namely, to increase the number of deputies; but my fear would be that that would make for too much agitation in the state and would come too close to the turbulence of a democracy. If it became absolutely necessary to alter the present ratio, I should favor reducing the number of senators rather than increasing the number of deputies. The more I think about it, moreover, the less I am able to see why, with a paladin at the head of each province, you need your grand castel-

[3] [What Rousseau means by this is anybody's guess.]

lans. But let us never lose sight of the important maxim: do not change anything, add nothing, subtract nothing, unless you have to.

It is better, to my mind, to have a smaller assembly, and allow its members greater freedom than to increase their number and limit free discussion, as one must do when an assembly grows too large. To which I shall add this: if you will let me think forward to good things as well as bad ones, you must avoid making the Diet as large as it might be, in order not to cut yourself off from the means by which, one day, you might without too much trouble make room for some new deputies if you ever decide to ennoble your towns and enfranchise your serfs as, for the sake of a stronger and happier Poland, it is desirable for you to do.

Let us, then, seek a remedy for the defect here in question in some other way, so as to change as little as possible.

Your senators are all appointed by the king and are, consequently, the king's creatures. However, they are also appointed for life, and in that sense stand over against the king, and the knightly order, as an independent body, with its own sectional interest, its own unavoidable tendency toward usurpation—and let no one accuse me of contradicting myself because I recognize the senate as a *separate body* [4] in the republic, but do not recognize it as a *constituent order* [5] of the republic: they are quite different things.

First, you must take away from the king the appointment of the senators, not so much because of the power over them that it leaves in his hands, which is perhaps not very great, but because of the power he exercises over all who aspire to be senators, and through them over the entire body of the nation. This reform, quite apart from the effect it will have upon your constitution, will have a further inestimable advantage: it will discourage the spirit of courtliness and awaken patriotism among the nobles. I myself do not see any objection to having your senators named by the Diet and should expect such an ar-

[4] [Italics added.]
[5] [Italics added.]

rangement to bring you great benefits, too obvious to require detailed explanation. You could either have the Diet elect them at a single stage, or there could be a preliminary election in the dietines, which would certify a certain number of names to the Diet for each vacancy in the several palatinates; or the Diet could select, from among the names certified to it, some smaller number and let the king then have the right of making the final choice. But why not proceed directly to the simplest method of all and have each paladin elected once and for all by the dietine of his province? What objection has there been to this mode of election for the paladins of Polock and Witebsk and the starost of Samogitie? And what harm would be done by making the privilege enjoyed by these three provinces a right shared by all the provinces? Let us never lose sight of how important it is for Poland to orient its constitution toward federalism, so as to avoid, as much as possible, the evils that attach to the great state, or rather to the state with a vast territory.

Second: if you provide that your senators shall not hold office for life, you will weaken considerably that corporate interest on the senate's part that tends toward usurpation. That, to be sure, is not going to be easy to do. For one thing, it is hard on a man who is in the habit of managing public affairs to find himself reduced, for no reason at all, to the status of private citizen. For another, your senate seats are linked both to the titles of paladin and castellan and to the local authority that attaches to them; and the continual passing of these titles and this authority from hand to hand would produce both confusion and discontentment. Finally, your bishops could not, and your ministers perhaps should not, be given term appointments: ministerial posts call for specific talents and are not always easy to fill in a satisfactory manner; and if the bishops alone had life tenure, the power of the clergy, already excessive, would be much increased. So you must see to it that their power is balanced by some senators appointed, like the bishops, for life and as little afraid as they are of being removed.

Here is what I should imagine to be a solution to all these

problems: I should like the appointments of senators of the highest rank to continue to be for life. That, if you included here not only the bishops and paladins but also all the castellans of the highest rank, would give you eighty-nine life-tenure senators. As for the castellans of the second rank, I should like them all to have terminal appointments, perhaps for two years, with each new Diet electing a new set, or, if that seemed advisable, for longer than two years, but with each appointment lapsing at the end of the period specified. This, however, is without prejudice to the Diet's re-electing any appointees it might wish to continue in office—which, however, I should permit to happen only a certain number of times, as in the plan I shall propose below.

As for the titles, they would not be much of an obstacle; they carry with them, to all intents and purposes, no function other than sitting in the senate, and no harm would be done by abolishing them, so that, instead of being called bench castellans, they would simply be called senator-deputies. And since your reformed senate, because vested with executive power, would sit continuously as represented by a certain number of its members, a fixed proportion of the senator-deputies would, by turns, need to be present at all times. But our business here is not with details of that kind.

Actually, the well-nigh imperceptible change I am proposing would transform the castellans, or rather the senator-deputies, into so many representatives in the Diet, where they balance the senate as a body and strengthen the hand of the knightly order in the nation's councils; so that the senators with life tenure, though more powerful than before—both because of abolishing the veto and because the power of the king and the power of the ministers, which is based in part on that of the senate, would be greatly reduced—would be unable to impose the senate's corporate point of view upon the Diet. And the senate itself, with half its members appointed for fixed terms and half for life, would be constituted in the best manner possible to serve as an intermediate power between the Diet and the king; it would be sufficiently stable to control the administration, yet sufficiently dependent to remain subordinated to the laws. This measure, simple and yet highly effective, strikes me as a good one.

I have said nothing thus far about how votes are to be counted. In an assembly of approximately three hundred members, this is a simple matter. In London, where the assembly is much larger than that, they manage to get them counted; in Geneva too, where the General Council is larger still and everyone breathes distrust; and, more surprisingly, even in Venice, where the Grand Council includes some twelve hundred nobles, and corruption and chicanery rule the roost. I have, for the rest, dealt with this matter in the *Social Contract;* and it is that book that the reader who is kind enough to value my opinion should consult.

It has been proposed, as a means of mitigating the abuses associated with the veto, that you stop polling the deputies' votes individually and count them henceforth by palatinates. You could not possibly think this reform over too carefully before adopting it, although it has its good points and is favorable to a federal form of government. Votes cast collectively, in blocs, invariably address themselves less directly to the common interest than votes cast individually, one at a time. Often the following will happen: among the deputies from a palatinate, as they deliberate, there will be one who will gain the ascendancy over the others, the majority voting as he votes, which it would not have done if the votes had been cast independently; so that the agents of corruption will have less work to do and know more certainly whom to approach. For the rest, it is better to have each of the deputies answering for himself to the dietines, so that none can put blame off on the others, so that the innocent will never be mistaken for the guilty, and so that distributive justice will be better observed. There are a great many arguments against this way of counting votes, the effect of which would be to weaken the common bond and, conceivably, expose the state to disruption in every Diet. By binding the deputies more tightly to their instructions and to their constituents, you will gain approximately the same benefits without any undesirable results whatever—assuming, to be sure, that votes will be cast *viva voce* and not by secret ballot, so that each deputy's actions and opinions will be matters of public knowledge, and that he will answer for them in person. But the whole business of voting is one of the questions to which I have given most careful attention in the *Social Contract*,[6] and there is no point in my repeating myself here.

As for your elections, the naming of so many senator-deputies, simultaneously in each Diet, may seem clumsy at first, to say nothing of, as a general proposition, the choosing of a large number of names out of a still larger number of names, which will happen from time to time under the plan I am proposing. But if you were to have recourse to the ballot, you could easily get around the difficulty by using printed cards, numbered serially, which would be distributed to the electors on the eve of the election. These cards would carry a complete list of the candidates to be voted on; and on the following day the electors, each having marked—in conformity with the instructions appearing at the top of the ballot—the names of the candidates he favors or opposes, would step forward one after another and deposit their respective cards in a hopper. The ballots would then be read off, immediately and in the presence of the assembly, by the Diet secretary, assisted by two other secretaries *ad actum* whom the marshal would name then and there from among the members in attendance. The operation, if handled in this way, would be so short and simple that the full complement of senators could be elected at a single sitting and without any disagreement or turmoil. You would, to be sure, also need rules for drawing up the list of candidates; but we shall keep that in mind and discuss it in its proper place.

It remains to speak of the king, who presides over the Diet and should, in virtue of his position, be the supreme administrator of the laws.

[6] IV, ii, iv.

VIII
CONCERNING
THE KING

It is a bad state of affairs when a nation has as its chief the born enemy of its liberty, of which he ought to be the defender. But the evil in question is not, in my view, inherent in the chief's office to such an extent that we cannot eliminate it, or at least considerably reduce it. Where there is no hope there is no temptation so that, if you make usurpation impossible for your kings, you will stop them from dreaming about it, and all the energies they now devote to enslaving you will go into governing you well and seeing to your defense.

Poland's original law-givers, as Count Wielhorski has pointed out, took pains to deprive your kings of the means of doing harm but not of the means of corrupting; and the favors that are theirs to bestow give them such means in abundance. Your present difficulty is this: to take away from them the capacity to bestow favors seems like taking everything away from them, which, however, is what you must not do: it would be tantamount to having no king at all, and I believe that no state as large as Poland can do without one—without, that is, a supreme chief with life tenure. Now: Either the chief of the nation is to be a complete cipher, and thus useless, or he must be in a position to do something. And that something, no matter how small, will necessarily be either good or evil. At the present time the king has the appointment of all the senators, which is too much power; while, if he had no share in their appointment, he would not have enough. Take the English peers: they also are royal appointees but less dependent on the crown than yours are, because their titles, once conferred, are hereditary. Your titles (bishop, paladin, and grand castellan), being for life only, revert to the Crown upon the death of each incumbent. I have already indicated how, in my opinion, they should be named: the paladins and grand castellans for life, and by their respective dietines; the lesser castellans for a specified number of years, and by the Diet. As for the bishops, it seems to me that you can hardly take their election away from the king, except to entrust it to their chapters; it would, I think, be just as well to leave it in his hands, except for the archbishopric of Guesne, which in the nature of the case belongs to the Diet—unless you separate it from the office of primate, which only the Diet should dispose of. As for the ministers, the ranking generals and treasury lords especially, their power, which balances that lodged in the king, ought, to be sure, to be reduced in the same proportion as his; and it would be imprudent, I think, to leave to the king the power to put his own creatures into such offices; so that I should prefer to leave him, at most, the privilege of choosing each appointee from a brief list of names to be certified to him by the Diet. I grant that he cannot revoke an appointment once he has made it, and therefore cannot count on the appointee to obey him in all matters. But the power the appointments give him over would-be appointees is power enough—if not to enable him to change the face of the government, at least to leave him the hope of doing so. And that hope, above all, is what you must take away from him at all costs.

As for the lord chancellor, he should, in my view, be appointed by the king. Kings are the born judges of their peoples; they were first established for that function, even if they have everywhere turned their backs on it; it cannot be taken away from them; and if they choose not to perform it themselves, the power of appointing those who are to substitute for them in this area is theirs as a matter of right, since it is they who must always answer for the judgments handed down in their name. The nation can, to be sure, give them assessors, and ought to do so when they do not themselves sit as judges; wherefore the Tribunal of the Crown, which is presided over not by the king but by the lord chancellor, is supervised by the nation, and it is only right that the dietines should appoint its other members. If, however, the king elected to try cases in person, I hold that he would have the right to try them without assessors. Alone or accompanied, he would always find it to his interest to act justly. For iniquitous judicial decisions have never been the high road to successful usurpation.

The remaining preferments, both in the royal household and in the palatinates, are merely honorific, and the titles they carry with them confer prestige rather than authority. The best you can do is let them remain entirely at the king's disposal. Leave the king free to honor merit and flatter vanity, but not to bestow power.

The majesty of the throne should have a splendid setting; but all the outlays that necessitates should be left as little as possible at the charge of the king. It would be desirable, indeed, to have all crown officials on the republic's payroll rather than on the king's list, and to reduce the king's revenues correspondingly, so as to reduce to a minimum the funds he actually handles.

It has been proposed that you make the crown hereditary. Be assured, however, that Poland can bid farewell forever to its freedom on the day such a law goes on the books. People think it is enough, in this regard, to place limitations on the king's power; what they overlook is that the limitations the laws impose will, as time passes, be got around by means of gradual usurpation, and that in the long run the over-all policy adopted and continuously pursued by the royal family will win out over the laws, the latter having an inherent tendency to lose their vigor. Even if the king cannot corrupt the grandees by bestowing favors, he can always corrupt them with promises to be redeemed by his successors; and since the plans developed by the royal family are perpetuated with it, people will put much more faith in its engagements, and rely much more strongly upon their fulfillment, than ever they would if an elective crown called attention to the fact that the monarch's projects will terminate with his life. Poland is free today because there each new reign is preceded by an interval during which the nation resumes all its rights and youthful vigor, and arrests the growth of abuses and usurpations, so that the laws rise again and recover their pristine energy. What will become of the *pacta conventa*, the buckler of Poland, when a single family is so established on the throne that it can hand it down continuously from son to son, leaving the nation, between the death of the father and the coronation of the son, nothing but the empty and meaningless shadow of liberty? That will soon destroy even that pretense of an oath that all your kings took in the past upon their coronation and dismissed from their minds forever a moment later. You saw what happened in Denmark, you see what is happening in England; and tomorrow you are going to see it happen in Sweden. You must profit from these examples, and learn, once and for all, that no matter how high you pile your precautions, a hereditary throne and a free nation are incompatible.

The Poles have always had a penchant for handing the crown down from father to son or next of kin, though always exercising their right of election. That practice—if they keep it up—will sooner or later lead to the evil day on which they will make the crown hereditary. They must not hope to maintain their struggle against royal power over a long period, like that of the members of the German Empire against the power of the emperor; for Poland does not have within it, at all, the counterweight a country must have if it is to keep a hereditary king subordinated to the laws. The Empire has several powerful members, but despite that fact, the imperial capitulations would be a vain formula, as they were at the beginning of the century, except for the accident of Charles VII's election. And your *pacta conventa* would be emptier still once your royal family had had time to consolidate its position and situate itself above all other families. Here, in a word, is my opinion on this topic: Poland would be better off with an elected king exercising the most absolute power, than with a hereditary king exercising almost no power at all.

Instead of this fateful statute that would make your crown hereditary, I should propose one that is quite the reverse, and that would, if you adopted it, preserve the liberty of Poland. It would provide, by fundamental law, that the crown would never pass from father to son, so that every son of a Polish king would be forever excluded from the throne. Or perhaps I should say that I should favor such a law if it were needed, but that I have a plan in mind that would accomplish the same result in another way. However, I reserve the explanation of this plan until a more appropriate moment, and, merely positing here that its effect would be to exclude the sons of the kings at least from immediate access to the throne, I record my belief that the preservation of your freedom will not be the only benefit their exclusion would confer. It would, rather, produce this further considerable advantage: by depriving your kings of all hope of usurping arbitrary power and transmitting it to their heirs, it would channel all their efforts into forwarding the glory and prosperity of the state, which would be the sole avenue left open to their ambition. The chief of the nation would then become, instead of its born enemy, its first citizen, and make it his chief concern to initiate improvements that would shed luster on his reign, win him the affection of his people and the respect of his neighbors, and cause his memory to be cherished after his death. And only then would you be well-advised, apart from the means of doing injury and corrupting officials, which you must never leave in his hands, to increase his powers—in all matters bearing upon the public good. He will have little immediate and direct power to act on his own, but much authority—to supervise and inspect in order to hold others within the limits set by their duties and to point the government toward its true purpose. Presiding over the Diet, the senate, and other public bodies; keeping a strict watch upon the conduct of all public servants; seeing to it that justice and integrity prevail in all the courts; preserving order and tranquillity within the state; assuring it a sound position vis-à-vis the outside world; commanding the armies in time of war and fostering improvements in time of peace—these are the tasks that properly belong to his royal office; and if he is willing to perform them in person, they will keep his hands full. The details of administration would be handled by ministers placed in office to see to them, so that it should be a crime for a king of Poland to hand over any part of his own functions to favorites. Let him work at his trade in person or else give it up. An important principle, on which the nation should never relax its vigilance.

Such are the principles that should govern the checks and balances among the several powers that enter into legislation and administration. These powers—in the hands of their depositaries and in their best possible relation to one another—should vary directly with the number of hands, and inversely with the length of time they remain in one set of hands. The component parts of the Diet will approximate this optimum relation fairly closely: The Chamber of Deputies, the more numerous of the two chambers, will also be the more powerful; but its entire membership will change frequently. The senate, which is smaller, will have a lesser share in legislation but a greater share of executive power; and its members, who will participate in the constitution on both extremes, will be partly men with life tenure and partly men with terminal appointments, which is an arrangement appropriate to an intermediate body. The king, who presides over everything, will continue to hold office for life; and his power, still very great where supervision is concerned, will be limited by the Chamber of Deputies as regards legislation, and by the senate as regards administration. In order to maintain equality, however, as the principle of your constitution, nothing should be hereditary save the nobility. If the crown were hereditary, you would have, for sake of balance, to make the peerage or senatorial order hereditary too, as in England, and then the knightly order, placed at a disadvantage, would lose the power it now exercises, since your Chamber of Deputies, unlike the House of Commons, does not open and close the public treasure-chest every year. In a word: the Polish constitution would be turned completely upside-down.

IX

SPECIFIC CAUSES
OF ANARCHY

The Diet, once balanced and moderated in the manner just described, will give you good laws and good administration. But it can do these things only if its commands are respected and obeyed.

The contempt for the laws, the anarchy, in which Poland has lived up to now, are easy to explain, and I have already directed attention to the most important of the causes for them and indicated the remedy. The other causes, complementary in character, are 1) the *liberum veto*, 2) the confederations, and 3) abuse by individuals of the right—which has not yet been taken away from them—to maintain their own troops.

The third of these abuses is of such character that all other reforms will prove useless unless it is eliminated to begin with. So long as there are individuals sufficiently powerful to resist the executive power, those individuals will feel they have the right to do so; and whilst they continue to fight their small wars against one another, how can one hope for peace within the state? Your strongholds require garrisons? I agree. But why do you need strongholds that are strong only against your citizens, and weak against your enemies?

The reform I propose will, I fear, run up against difficulties; but these I do not believe to be insuperable. Even the most unreasonable of your more powerful citizens will willingly consent to give up his private army when nobody else has one.

I propose to speak later of your military establishment, and to postpone, for the moment, certain things that I might otherwise have said in the present chapter.

The *liberum veto*, not a bad thing in and of itself, becomes the most dangerous of abuses when it exceeds certain limits. Once the bulwark of your political freedom, it is today merely the instrument of your oppression; and the only means you still have of ridding yourselves of this fatal abuse is to root out completely anything that produces it. There is, to be sure, something in the heart of man that clings more stubbornly to individual privileges than to those advantages that, though greater, are less exclusive; nor can anything save patriotism, enlightened by experience, teach him to give up, in favor of greater goods, a once-glorious right that has become pernicious through abuse and is now inseparable from that abuse. No Pole can be unaware of the misfortunes this ill-omened right has brought upon all the Poles; and if they love law and order, they have no means of establishing either while they permit its exercise. When the body politic is in process of being formed, or where it has achieved its full development, the *liberum veto* is a good thing; but while there are reforms still to be effected, it is absurd and can result only in disaster. And it is impossible, especially since yours is a large state surrounded by powerful and ambitious neighbors, that you do not have reforms still to be carried out.

Your *liberum veto* would be less unreasonable if it applied only to the fundamental provisions of your constitution; for it to apply indiscriminately to every decision of the Diet, however, is inadmissible from every point of view. One of the vices of the Polish constitution is that it does not distinguish clearly enough between legislation and administration. Your Diet, mixing in bits of administration with its exercise of legislative power, performs indifferently acts of government and acts of sovereignty; often, indeed, it performs mixed acts, which make its members administrators and legislators at one and the same time.

The reforms I have proposed make, accordingly, for a sharper distinction between the two powers, and, by the same token, for a clearer demarcation of the limits of the *liberum veto*. I assume, for this purpose, that it never entered anybody's head to extend the veto to purely administrative matters. That would mean the extinction of civil authority and of the entire government.

In accordance with the natural right of societies, unanimity was required both for the establishment of your body politic and for the fundamental laws that bear directly upon its very existence—for example, the first as amended, the fifth, the ninth, and eleventh of the laws approved by the pseudo-Diet of 1768. The unanimity that was required for the adoption of these laws should likewise be required for their abrogation. Here, then, are some matters to which the *liberum veto* can continue to apply, so that what is in question here is not its complete abolition; and the Poles, who did not kick up much fuss when the veto was restricted in the pseudo-Diet of 1768, ought not to complain at its being curtailed and hedged about in a Diet whose freedom and legitimacy are less open to question.

You must give careful thought to the capital provisions that are to be established as fundamental law, and then have the *liberum veto* apply exclusively to those provisions. You will then have given your constitution as firm a basis, and will have made your fundamental laws as nearly irrevocable, as you possibly can. My reasoning here is this: it is contrary to the nature of the body politic for it to impose laws upon itself that it cannot repeal. But it is not contrary to nature, or to reason, for it to be unable to repeal those same laws except with the same solemn procedures that were used for their adoption. That is the one fetter the body politic can place upon itself as regards the future. Nor is any further limitation needed, either to shore up your constitution or to indulge the Poles' love for the *liberum veto* and yet not to expose them further to the abuses to which it has given rise.

As for all those other provisions, which in Poland have been declared fundamental although they are mere statutes, and those that are brought together under the general heading "matters of state," both are subject, because of the changeableness of things, to necessary modifications that do not admit of the unanimity requirement. Here it is absurd, whatever the circumstances, for a single member to be able to bring the Diet's activities to a stop, or for the withdrawal or protest of a single deputy, or even several deputies, to dissolve the assembly and so annul the authority of the sovereign. You must abolish the barbarous right that makes these things possible, and punish by death any man who might be tempted to exercise it. Even assuming that there are occasions for protest against the Diet, which is impossible so long as the Diet is free and has its full complement of deputies, the right to protest could be vested only in the palatinates and the dietines and never in the individual deputies. The latter, as members of the Diet, should not have the slightest power over it and should never challenge its decisions.

The veto, which represents the maximum of power on the part of the individual members of the Diet, should come into play only with respect to genuinely fundamental laws. The majority principle, which represents the minimum of power on the part of the individual members, should apply to matters of a purely administrative character. In between the two, however, there are variations that, depending on the importance of the questions being voted on, may be taken as determining the preponderance of votes. For laws, for instance, you might require at least a three-fourths majority of the votes cast; for matters of state, two-thirds; for elections, and for other matters that are either routine or of momentary interest, a simple majority. These are only examples with which to illustrate the idea, not a series of ratios that I commit myself to.

In a state like Poland, where men's souls still retain great vigor, it might at one time have been possible to preserve the glorious right to the *liberum veto* without too great a risk and perhaps even to good purpose. But only on one condition, namely, that the right be made dangerous to exercise, by attaching to it grave consequences for the individual availing himself of it. It is preposterous, I make bold to say, for the man who thus arrests the activities of the Diet, leaving the state helpless, to be able to go off home and rejoice, tranquilly, with impunity, in the public misfortune he has brought about.

If, then, the individual dissident member were to retain the right to annul an almost unanimous resolution of the Diet, I should wish that member to answer for his opposition with his head—not merely to his own constituents in the post-session dietine, but also, at a later date, to the entire nation upon which he has brought disaster. Concretely, I should like the law to provide as follows: six months after his exercise of the veto, let him be solemnly judged by a special tribunal, established for this very purpose, which would be made up of all the nation's wisest, most illustrious, and most respected citizens. Let that tribunal not be empowered to send him on his way with a simple acquittal. Let it be required, rather, to condemn him to death without mercy, or else to bestow a reward upon him and, along with it, public honors for the rest of his life, without any middle course between these alternatives ever being open to the tribunal.

Arrangements like the one I have just described are highly favorable to vigor of spirit and love of liberty, but are too foreign to modern hearts and minds for one to expect them to be adopted—or even admired. Among the ancients, however, they were by no means unknown: they were, rather, the means by which their founders were able to lift up men's souls and set them afire, in time of need, with truly heroic zeal. Their history tells of public-spirited citizens, in republics with even harsher laws than that just mentioned, who, when the fatherland was in danger, risked death in order to force discussion of a proposal that might save it. The veto, with that same risk attached to it, may some day save your state, and will never be a matter for great fears.

Do I dare say a word here, in the teeth of the authorities,

about the confederations? The authorities see only the evil the confederations do; but one must take into account also the evil they prevent. The confederation is, indisputably, an interval of violence in the life of the republic; but there are diseases so ravaging as to render violent remedies necessary, and we must attempt to stamp out these diseases at any price whatever. The confederation is to the Poles what the dictatorship was to the Romans; both silence the laws in times of pressing danger, but with this great difference: the dictatorship, which was repugnant both to the laws of Rome and to the spirit of its government, finally destroyed that government. The confederations, by contrast, since they are merely a means for mobilizing great energies to fortify and restore the constitution when it has been shaken, are capable of tightening and strengthening the slackened spring of the state, but not of breaking it. The federative device, for all that it may have originated quite fortuitously, seems to me a political masterpiece. Liberty—wherever it prevails—is constantly under attack, and very often in real danger; and any free state in which men have failed to think forward to the great crisis is threatened with extinction each time a storm breaks out. Only the Poles have been able to extract from these very crises a new means of preserving the constitution. Without the confederations the republic of Poland would long ago have ceased to exist; and I greatly fear that it will not long survive the confederations should you decide to abolish them. Look at what has just happened. The state, but for the confederations, would have been subjugated; your liberty would have been destroyed forever. Do you wish to strip the republic of the very resource that has just saved it from extinction?

And let no one tell himself that the confederations will become useless once the *liberum veto* is abolished and the majority-principle reinstated—as if the confederations afforded no advantage beyond that principle. This is to confuse matters. The confederations, because of the executive power they carry with them, will always possess—in moments of dire need—a vigor, a capacity to act and act quickly, that are out of the question for the Diet for this reason: it must proceed more deliberately, with great formality, and cannot do anything irregular without upsetting the constitution. The confederations are the buckler, the refuge, the sanctuary, of your constitution. So long as the confederations remain alive the constitution cannot, I believe, destroy itself. You must retain them; but you must also lay down rules for them. If all existing abuses were eliminated, the confederations would become well-nigh useless; and since the reform of your government should eliminate the abuses, there will remain, as occasions for necessary resort to confederations, only outbreaks of violence. But outbreaks of violence belong to the category of things you must think forward to. Instead of abolishing the confederations, then, define the situations in which they may legitimately take place; then lay down clear rules regarding their form and function, so as to give them legal sanction, to the extent that this is possible without putting obstacles in the way of their formation or their activity. There are, I should say, situations whose mere existence calls for the instant confederation of all Poland. For example, when the troops of a foreign power—on whatever pretext, and not exclusively in the case of open war—set foot on Polish soil. Whatever the occasion for their entry, including the consent of the Polish government itself, confederating on one's own territory is not a hostile act against another country. Whenever—be the obstacle what it may—the Diet is prevented from assembling on the day fixed by law; whenever—be the responsible party who he may—troops have been stationed at its meeting-place when it is to convene; whenever the Diet's structure is changed or its deliberations suspended or its freedom curtailed in any way—in all these cases a nation-wide confederation should come into existence as a matter of course. Regional assemblies and local committees are merely branches of the nation-wide confederation, and their marshals should all be subordinated to whoever has been named premier.

X

ADMINISTRATION

I am going to leave aside administrative details, about which I possess neither knowledge nor opinions, and venture some comments on only two of its phases: finance and war. I feel fairly certain that the things I shall say will not appeal to you, but since I deem them sound I see nothing for it but to include them. First of all, however, I propose to say a word or two—somewhat more in keeping with the spirit of the government of Poland—concerning the administration of justice.

The ancients knew neither the long robe nor the sword as professional callings: their citizens did not "become" soldiers or judges or priests, but served in each of the capacities as duty required. There you have the true secret of making everything move toward a common goal, of seeing to it that occupational loyalties put down no roots at the expense of patriotism, and of making sure that the hydra of chicanery shall make no feast upon the body of the nation. Service as a judge, whether in your highest tribunals or in your local courts, should be short-term service—a testing-time by means of which the nation can form a judgment regarding the citizen's merit and probity, with a view to promoting him, later, to such posts of greater eminence as he may be deemed capable of fulfilling. So the judges themselves should think of it; that will make them take great care not to throw themselves open to any possible reproach and will develop in them, at least usually, all the scrupulousness and integrity their office calls for. Such is the way men rose, in the great days in Rome, through the praetorship to the consulate; and if you adopt a similar arrangement yourselves, at the same time empowering your judges to interpret and amplify your laws, where necessary, according to the lights of their native rectitude and good sense, then Poland will, with a few clear, simple laws and a bare handful of judges, have its justice well administered. Nothing could be more childish than the precautions the English take in this matter. In the hope of excluding arbitrariness from their courts they have let themselves in for an endless round of decisions, ranging all the way from the iniquitous to the fantastic. Swarms of lawyers prey upon them, and interminable lawsuits consume them. In a mad attempt to provide for everything beforehand, they have made their laws an immense labyrinth, in which memory and reason alike lose their way.

You must draw up three codes: one for your political laws, one for your civil laws, and one for your criminal laws. All three ought to be as clear, brief, and precise as you can make them; and they should be taught not only in your universities but in all your colleges as well. Nor will you need any fourth or fifth body of laws. The rules of natural right can all be read more clearly in men's own hearts than in any hodge-podge got together by Justinian; [1] only make those hearts

[1] [Cf. *Social Contract*, II, xii ("Classification of the Laws"), where, as here, Rousseau also offers a four-fold classification: political or fundamental laws, civil laws, criminal laws, and a fourth type of laws which—a matter of great interest for our purposes—he identifies not by putting a name to them, but by saying where they are to be found: "Laws of this type are engraved not upon tablets of marble or brass, but upon the hearts of the citizens. These laws it is that, acquiring new vigor with each passing day, make up the state's real constitution. . . . It is they that keep a people within the spirit of its institutions, and gradually substitute the force of habit for the force of authority. I refer to the people's mores, to their customs, above all to their opinions, *thus to an aspect* (of the body politic) *that our political theorists ignore. . . . This is the aspect over which the great legis-*

honest and virtuous, and I promise you their owners will know
all the law they will need. As for the positive enactments of
the land, however, your citizens, particularly those who are
active in public affairs, should receive instruction about them,
as also about the specific laws under which they are governed. These they would find in the codes they would be required to study; and each noble should stand an examination
on the three codes, the political code in particular, before his
name is inscribed in the Golden Book that opens to him the
doors of his dietine. This examination, furthermore, should be
no mere formality; if he has not sufficiently mastered the
codes, he should be sent home to study them again. As for
Roman law and customary law, both, if you now have them,
should be banned from your courts and schools alike, neither
of which should recognize any authority other than Poland's
own laws. The latter, so as to seal off at least one source of liti-
gation, should be made uniform throughout the provinces; and
any question not covered by the laws should be left to the
good sense and integrity of your judges. You may depend
upon it that when the incumbent of each judgeship regards it
as a test to be met in order to win promotion, such power as
this gives him will not be abused in the way that one might
otherwise fear. Even if it were, however, the abuse would be
smaller than abuses associated with a multitude of laws,
which are these: the laws often come into conflict with one
another; their very number makes for endless lawsuits;
and, insofar as they do contradict one another, they make for
unpredictable decisions.

All that I say here about your judges applies with even
greater force to your advocates. Their function too is one that

---

lator broods in secret. . . . (Particular) enactments . . . are . . .
merely the arc of the arch, while the mores, which demand more
patient midwifery, emerge finally as its unshakable keystone"
(italics added). The questions arise imperatively: Why does the
author of the *Government of Poland* know of a law or right of
nature, while the author of the *Social Contract* does *not* know of
it? Note that both types of law are engraved upon, or to be read
in, the "hearts of the citizens."]

merits profound respect and is cheapened and debased when it becomes a calling. The advocate should be his client's first and most severe judge; his position should be—as it was in Rome, and is still in Geneva—the first rung on a ladder that leads to the magistracy. In Geneva advocates are held in high regard, and deservedly so, for they are all candidates for membership in the council, and are thus scrupulously careful to do nothing that might run them afoul of public opinion. I should like every public office to lead in this fashion to another, so that nobody would be pulling wires to keep the one he has and, by developing it into a lucrative occupation, make himself independent of the verdict of others on his performance. This would serve perfectly the purpose of forcing the sons of your rich men to pass through the post of advocate, now made over into one of honor but of brief tenure. I shall develop this notion more fully in a moment.

I must point out in passing—since it comes to mind in this connection—that both entails and primogeniture are contrary to the principle of equality within the knightly order. The tendency of your laws should be toward a continuous reduction of large inequalities of wealth and power, since it is these that are responsible for the excessively wide chasm between your great lords and your ordinary nobles—a chasm that the cumulative operation of natural forces tends unavoidably to widen further. As regards, however, a property qualification for admission to the dietines, which would stipulate a certain amount of land each noble would be required to own for that purpose, I see something to be said both for and against it; and since I am not sufficiently familiar with your country to estimate its effects, I shall not venture to decide the issue at all. No one can deny that it would be desirable for every citizen who votes in a palatinate to own land in it. On the other hand, I am not greatly attracted to the idea of stipulating the *amount* [2] of land. Are we to let possessions count for so much that men will count for nothing? Is a man really the less noble—or the less free—because he owns only a tiny patch of

[2] [Italics added.]

land, or no land at all? Is his poverty really so grave a crime as to cost him his rights as a citizen?

One final word: never permit one of your laws to fall into desuetude, not even a law that does not matter one way or the other; not even if it is downright bad. This principle—either formal repeal or full enforcement—is fundamental; and it means that you must review all your old laws, rescind a great many of them, and back up those you wish to retain with the severest possible sanctions. In France, it is a first principle of government that one must wink at many things—which is what despotism invariably obliges us to do. In a free governmental system, however, that is *the* [3] means of weakening the laws and undermining the constitution. The laws should be few in number. They should be well digested. They should, above all, be scrupulously obeyed. An abuse that is not yet forbidden by law is a matter of small importance; but the man who says "law" in a free state utters a word in the presence of which every citizen trembles—and the king first of all. In short: bear whatever misfortunes you must, but do not wear down the spring that gives force to your laws. For once it is spent the state is lost beyond recovery.

[3] [Italics added.]

XI

THE ECONOMIC
SYSTEM

Poland's policy as regards its economic system should depend on the purpose it sets itself in remodeling its constitution.

If what you wish is merely to make a great splash, to be impressive and formidable, to influence the other peoples of Europe, you have before you their example: get busy and imitate it. Cultivate the sciences, the arts, commerce, industry; have regular troops, fortified places, academies, and, above all, a fine financial system, which will make money circulate smoothly and so multiply and greatly enrich you. Strive to render money absolutely necessary so as to keep your people highly dependent—which calls also for fomenting material luxury and the luxury of the spirit that is inseparable from it. Do all this, and you will end up with a people as scheming, violent, greedy, ambitious, servile, and knavish as the next, and all of it at one extreme or the other of misery and opulence, of license and slavery, with nothing in between. You will, however, be accounted one of the great powers of Europe; you will take part in all its political systems; when negotiations are in progress, you will be sought after as an ally; you will be tied to other peoples by treaties; and you will have the honor of being dragged into every war fought in Europe. Nor is that all: should fortune damn you with her bounties, you will be able to recover your former possessions, perhaps even to conquer some new ones; and then—like Pyrrhus, like the Russians, which is to say like little children—you will be able to say: "When the world is mine, I am going to eat lots and lots of candy."

But if perchance you wish to be a free nation, a peaceful nation, a wise nation, a nation that fears nobody and needs nobody, a nation that is sufficient unto itself and happy, then you must use another method altogether, namely this: keep alive—or bring back to life—simple customs, wholesome tastes, and a spirit that is martial but not ambitious. Instill courage and unselfishness into the hearts of your people. Employ the masses of your population in agriculture and the arts necessary for life. Cause money to become an object of contempt and, if possible, useless besides; and make it your business, with an eye to the great things you are to accomplish, to discover some more powerful and dependable incentive. As you travel this path, to be sure, the reports of your celebrations, your negotiations, and your exploits will fill no newspapers. No philosophers will fawn upon you. No poets will write songs about you. You will seldom be the talk of Europe, which may even profess to view you with disdain. You will live, however, in an atmosphere of true abundance, of justice, and of freedom. No one will pick quarrels with you. People will, rather, fear you, while pretending not to. And I answer for it that neither the Russians nor anyone else will ever again come to Poland to lord it over you—or, should they make any such mistake, that they will get back out faster than they came in.

Since the two plans of action I speak of are for the most part mutually exclusive, you must, above all, not try to combine them. By attempting both, through some sort of mixed policy, you would cut yourselves off from success with either. Choose the one or the other, then. But if you prefer the first, do not read what follows; for all the proposals I have still to offer relate exclusively to the second.

Some of the economic designs set forth in the papers that have been sent to me are undoubtedly sound. But I find in them this defect: they are more likely to make you rich than to make you prosperous. One must look beyond the short-term effects of any projected improvement, and anticipate its unavoidable long-term effects. Take, for example, the proposal that you sell the starosties and use the proceeds in such and such a manner. It seems to me both well thought out and easy to carry through—within the assumptions of the system, now established all over Europe, under which one does everything with money. But what of this system itself? Is it sound? Does it really forward the purpose for which it is intended? Is it indeed certain that money is the sinews of war? Rich peoples, in point of fact, have always been beaten and taken over by poor peoples. Is it certain that money is what keeps things going in a good government? Systems of finance are a modern invention; they have produced nothing, so far as I can see, that is good or great either. The governments of ancient times were ignorant of the very word "finance," and yet they accomplished things with men that are wonderful to contemplate. Money, at best, merely supplements men; and that which supplements is never so valuable as that which is supplemented. Poles, do this for me: let the others have all the money in the world, or at least content yourselves with such of it as the others—since they need your wheat more than you need their gold—will find it necessary to give you. Believe me: to live abundantly is better than to live opulently. Be better off than mere wealth will ever make you, by providing yourselves with plenty. Tend your fields, and do not bother your heads about other things. You will harvest your gold soon enough, and in larger amounts than you need for the oil and wine you want. For, with those exceptions, Poland has in quantity—or is in position to produce—pretty much everything it requires.

Heads and hearts and hands are what you need to keep yourselves happy and free; they are the makings of a strong state and a prosperous people. Systems of finance produce venal hearts; for once a man makes up his mind that he is interested only in gain, he profits more by playing the knave than by being an honest man. Where money is used, it is easily diverted and concealed; what is intended for one purpose is utilized for another; those who handle money soon learn how to divert it—and what are all the officials assigned to keep watch on them, except so many more rascals whom one sends along to go shares with them? If all riches were public and obvious, if gold, in moving from place to place, left behind it visible traces that were impossible to conceal, money would be the most convenient instrument there could be for purchasing services, courage, fidelity, virtues. Actually, however, it circulates secretly, and so lends itself even better to the making of thieves and traitors and the auctioning off of liberty and the public good. In a word, money is the weakest and least dependable engine I know of for driving the political machine toward its object, the strongest and surest for sending it off on a tangent.

One can make men act only by appealing to their self-interest. That I know. Of all interests, however, that in pecuniary gain is the most evil, the most vile, the readiest to be corrupted, though also—in the eyes of one who has knowledge of the human heart (I reiterate this with confidence and shall always insist upon it)—the least important and compelling. In the heart of every man there is a natural reservoir of several strong passions: if in any man only the passion for money remains alive, that is because the remaining passions, which should have been awakened and developed in him, have been starved or stamped out. The true miser, properly speaking, has no dominant passion at all; he hoards money only by way of looking ahead, in order to gratify such passions as may arise in him later. Learn how to foment these passions, learn how to open up a direct path to their satisfaction that can be travelled without money, and money will soon lose its price.

What of the expenses incurred by the state—are they not unavoidable? Agreed again; defray them any way you like, except with money. In Switzerland, one sees, even today, officials and magistrates and other public employees being paid in kind, that is, in the form of tithes, wine, wood, privileges, both utilitarian and honorific. All public services in that country are discharged by conscripted labor, and the state has little or no occasion to pay for anything in money. But, someone will object, they must have money with which to pay their troops. That question I shall return to in a minute.

The method of payment I have just spoken of is not without disadvantages. It entails waste and extravagance. It is clumsy to administer. It is, above all, distasteful to administrators, who have a hard time making a good thing out of it. All that is true. But how small all that is in comparison to the multiplicity of evils it prevents! Try as a man may to make off with something, he still cannot do it—not, at least, without someone's seeing him.

What, someone may object, about the bailiffs in some Swiss cantons? But what is the source of annoyance here but the fact that they levy fines in money? The fines in question are, to be sure, arbitrary, and so highly objectionable per se. Even so, they would be a small matter if they could be collected only in goods. When that which is extorted is money, it is easily concealed; stores of commodities cannot be concealed to anything like the same extent. Ten times as much money is handled in Berne as in all the rest of Switzerland put together, and administration in Berne, in consequence, is ten times as iniquitous. Look at any country, at any form of government, at any estate. You will find no great evil, whether in morals or in politics, in which money does not play a part.

· Outlays for administration, someone will say, can easily be held down in Switzerland because there wealth is evenly distributed; while Poland, by contrast, has its powerful families and great lords, whose maintenance calls for large expenditures and thus for ready cash. Nothing of the kind. The wealth of your magnates is in the form of inherited estates; and once luxury has ceased to be held in honor in the state, their outlays will be smaller than at present, though still large enough to set them apart from the men of lesser wealth, since the latter will reduce their outlays in the same proportion. The great lords' services should be paid for with authority, honors, and high office. With you, inequality of rank is offset by the advantage always conferred by a nobility, namely, that the holders of the various ranks are more avid of honors than of gain. Your republic has but to graduate and allocate its purely honorific rewards wisely, and it will have at its disposal a treasury that not only will never bankrupt it but will give it heroes for citizens. A treasury of honors is an inexhaustible resource for any people with a sense of honor. May God grant to Poland, then, the hope of exhausting it! Happy that nation that has bestowed the last possible distinction upon virtue!

Besides being unworthy of Poland, pecuniary rewards have this disadvantage: they are not public enough, and do not address themselves constantly to people's eyes and hearts; they disappear as soon as they are conferred, and so leave behind them no visible trace that, by perpetuating the honor that ought to attach to them, evokes emulation. I should like each rank, each employment, each honorific reward, to be dignified with its own external badge or emblem. I should like you to permit no office-holder to move about *incognito*, so that the marks of a man's rank or position shall accompany him wherever he goes; everyone should always show him respect, and he should never fail to maintain his self-respect. I should like the office-holder always to have the whip-hand over wealth—so much so that the rich man who is merely rich shall enjoy neither deference nor approval in his fatherland and shall find himself constantly over-shadowed by poor citizens upon whom titles have been conferred. If the rich man wishes to shine in his fatherland, let him have no choice but to serve it, to be upright for ambition's sake, and to aspire, for all that he is wealthy, to posts that only public approbation can bestow on him and that public blame can take away from him at a moment's notice. That is the way to sap the power of wealth and to produce men whom money cannot buy. I emphasize this point strongly, since I am deeply convinced that your neighbors, most especially the Russians, will do everything possible to corrupt your office-holders. Your government's first concern, therefore, must be to do what it can to make them incorruptible. Someone may object that I am trying to turn Poland into a nation of Capuchins. My first answer would be that this is an argument in the French manner and that wit and reason are by no means the same thing. My second answer would be that the principles I am urging must not be pushed beyond reasonable limits, or further than I intend. My purpose is not to abolish the circulation of money but to slow it down—and, above all, to show how important it is, if you are to have a good economic system, not to base it on finance and money. Lycurgus, in attempting to stamp out cupidity in Sparta, did not entirely eliminate money: he simply had it made out of iron. As for myself, I do not propose to proscribe silver or gold, but to make them play a less crucial role, and to see to it that the man who lacks both can be poor without being wretched as well. Money, in the last analysis, is not wealth, but merely an evidence of wealth; and what you must multiply is not the evidence of wealth but rather the thing itself. Take the English, surrounded as they are by all their gold; despite the tales told by travellers, they are not, man for man, one whit less hard up than other peoples. That I have seen with my own eyes. What good does it do me, after all, to have a hundred guineas, instead of only ten, if my hundred guineas will not buy me better keep? Pecuniary wealth is purely relative. According to the circumstances (which may change for any of ten thousand reasons), one can, with one and the same amount of money, be rich one moment and poor the next. But with one and the same amount of real goods, no such thing can happen; they are directly useful to man, and so have always an absolute value that the operations of the market cannot affect. The English people, I agree, is wealthier than any other. But it does not follow that a London burgher lives better than a Paris burgher. Nation for nation, the one with more money has an edge over that with less. But that tells us nothing about the lot of its individual members, because the prosperity of a nation does not depend upon money.

Foment agriculture and the useful arts—not by enriching the farmers, which will merely encourage them to stop being farmers, but by making their condition honorable and pleasant. Build shops of your own to produce everyday necessities; and—without giving other things a second thought—constantly expand both your wheat production and your population. Europe's increasingly numerous monopolies will see to it that the surplus produce of your land will be in short supply there; and that produce will, as a matter of course, bring you more money than you need. By trying to exceed that necessary and certain revenue, you will only make yourselves poorer; and once you have learned to do without it, you will be truly rich.

This, then, is the state of mind I should like to see dominate your economic system: scant preoccupation with the outside world, scant concern about trade, as much emphasis as possible on the multiplication of real goods and consumers. Under a free and equitable form of government, population increases unavoidably, naturally; so that the more you perfect your government, the more you will increase your population, even without setting yourselves that objective. You will have, as a result, neither beggars nor millionaires; luxury and indigence will disappear simultaneously, without your even noticing it. And the citizens, rescued both from the frivolous indulgences that riches encourage and the vices that misery brings in its train, will devote their energies and their ambition to serving the fatherland well—and will find their happiness in the performance of their duties.

I should like, I say, for your taxes to fall always upon men's backs more than upon their pocketbooks; for the work on your roads and bridges and public buildings, all services to the government and the state, to be performed by conscripted labor and not paid for in money. That, in the last analysis, is the least burdensome kind of tax; above all, it is the kind least open to abuse. For money, as it leaves the hand of the man who pays it over, vanishes from sight; while with men, everyone can see what use they are being put to. Nobody, therefore, can overburden them without good reason.

I realize that this way of handling the problem is impracticable where luxury, commerce, and the arts have carried the day. But for a simple people, with wholesome customs, it is the easiest way, and that most apt to keep its customs wholesome. Which is a still further reason for preferring it.

I return now to the question of the starosties. Let me, first of all, concede this: the proposal that you sell them and pay the proceeds into the public treasury is sound and well-considered from the standpoint of economics. But from the political and moral standpoint, it is so little to my liking that, had the starosties already been sold, I should favor buying them back—in order to convert them into a trust from which to draw pensions and rewards for those who have served the fatherland or deserved well of it. In a word: I should like you—if possible—to have no public treasury, but rather a taxing authority that would not so much as recognize payments in money. I do not have to be told, of course, that strict application of this principle is impossible. But the policy of your government should be oriented toward making it possible, and nothing could be more out of keeping with such a policy than the sale here in question. It would, to be sure, make your republic richer; but it would correspondingly weaken the spring from which your government draws its energies.

Administering the state's assets would, I grant, be more difficult—and less to the liking of the administrators—if payment were made in kind rather than in money. You must, however, make of the administrators' task, and of the post-audit of their work as well, still further tests of the good sense, the vigilance, and, above all, the integrity of which a man must give evidence before rising to posts of greater eminence. Here you will simply be following the example of the municipal administration of Lyons, where the man who wishes to win high municipal office must begin his career as administrator of the municipal hospital for the poor and is judged worthy of preferment in terms of his performance in that capacity. Nowhere, I might add, have there been more upright officials than the quaestors of the Roman armies, and for good reason, namely, the post of quaestor was a first step toward the curule offices.

A word now concerning the posts that offer temptations to the acquisitive. Here you must see to it that the incumbents' own ambitions apply the needed restraints. Nor will the prevention of graft be the greatest of the benefits you will derive from doing so. For you will also cause disinterestedness to be held in honor, and poverty—the kind of poverty that is the fruit of integrity—to be respected.

The republic's expenses exceed its revenues? Naturally, the citizens would prefer not to pay up at all. But men who would be free should not be slaves of their pocketbooks—for where is the state where liberty does not come at a price, and a high one at that? Switzerland? But the citizens of that country, as I have already pointed out, perform in person the functions that citizens of other countries prefer to pay others to perform: they take turns as soldiers, officers, magistrates, and workers, serving the state in whatever capacity it requires; and since they are always ready to honor drafts upon their persons they have no need to honor drafts upon their pocketbooks as well. The Poles, should they choose to follow that example, will have as little need of money as the Swiss. But the large state that refuses to act upon the principles of the small republic must not expect to enjoy the advantages those principles confer; it must not demand the result and reject the means of achieving it. If Poland were what I should like it to be, namely, a confederation of thirty-three tiny states, it would combine the strength of a great monarchy with the freedom of a small republic. But first you would have to renounce ostentation, and that, I fear, is the most difficult step of all.

The most convenient and inexpensive method for assessing taxes is, indisputably, capitation. It is also, however, the most unnatural and arbitrary method, which, no doubt, is why Montesquieu describes it as servile. Yet the Romans used it to the exclusion of all other methods, and right now it is in use, under a variety of names, in several republics: in Geneva, for example, where it is called "paying the watch." (Only citizens and burghers pay it; there are other taxes for the inhabitants and natives. Montesquieu would wish it the other way 'round.) [1]

To tax those who have nothing is both foolish and unjust. Taxes on things are, therefore, always preferable to taxes on persons, except that one must avoid taxes that are hard or costly to collect or—the important point—easy to evade by smuggling. Smuggling reduces revenue, fills the state with sharpers and thieves, and undermines the loyalty of its citizens.

Taxes should be so skillfully devised as to make fraud more trouble than it is worth. You must, therefore, never tax things that are easily hidden, such as lace or jewels; strike rather at the wearing of such things than at their importation. In France, they do everything they can to encourage smuggling, the tax-farmers apparently finding it to their interest to keep the smugglers in business—which is both contemptible and absurd.

As for stamp taxes, experience teaches us that they are especially burdensome to the poor, and that they interfere with trade, promote sharp practices, and evoke loud popular complaint wherever they are adopted. I advise you, therefore, not to give them a moment's thought. The tax on beasts of burden—provided steps are taken to prevent fraud, the very opportunity for which is a source of evils—seems to me much less objectionable. But it also, since it must be paid in money, can bear heavily upon the taxpayer; and the yield of any tax paid in money is too easily diverted from its proper channels.

The best tax, the least unnatural one, and the one that is proof against fraudulent evasion is, in my opinion, the proportional tax on land—all land, without exemptions of any kind—as proposed by Marshal Vauban and the Abbé de Saint Pierre. Production, after all is said and done, must foot the bills. All real estate—the king's, the nobles', the church's, the yeomen's—should pay at the same rate, namely, in proportion to area and yield, without distinction among classes of owners.

[1] [Parentheses added.]

Such a tax would, to be sure, seem to require as a matter of course a long and costly preliminary operation, to wit, a general land-survey. But that expense could be avoided quite easily and perhaps even beneficially, by assessing the tax on the product of the land rather than on the land itself, that is, by levying—at whatever rate seemed called for—upon the crops themselves, and taking payment, as with ecclesiastical tithes, in kind. This mode of assessment would, moreover, be even more equitable; and you could side-step such nuisances as handling small quantities and furnishing storage facilities by auctioning off the collection of levies, as the priests do with theirs. Each taxpayer, under such a scheme, would be accountable only for a certain fraction of his actual crop, and he would pay out of his pocket only when he himself, upon consulting the schedule fixed by the government, chose to do so. The proceeds of the tax could be pooled and utilized in your foreign commerce; that is, the commodities it would yield could be sold, and then shipped abroad via Danzig or Riga.

By adopting this plan you would spare yourselves all the expense of collection and administration and all those swarms of clerks and functionaries that are so distasteful to the people and so troublesome to the state. And, most important of all, the republic would have its money without the citizens' needing to fork it over. I cannot repeat too often that the tiller of the soil groans under the burden of the poll-tax, and other personal taxes also, because they are paid in money, and he must sell something in order to meet them.

XII

THE MILITARY
SYSTEM

The republic's largest outlays are those for the maintenance of
the crown's army, which are surely out of proportion to the
services it renders.

But, someone will reply at once, we must have troops to
defend the state; and if your troops *were* [1] defending the state,
I should not press my point. But I see no evidence that your
army has ever turned back an invader; and I am much afraid
that it will not defend you any better in the future.

Poland is surrounded by warlike powers, all of which
keep large numbers of admirably-disciplined troops ready for
action at all times. Try as it may, Poland will never be able
to match those troops without quickly exhausting its
resources—particularly while it is in the sorry state in which
the brigands now ravishing it are going to leave it. Moreover,
other powers will not permit it freedom of action. Let it,
utilizing the resources of the most vigorous possible administration, so much as try to put its army on a respectable
war footing, and its neighbors, determined as they are to prevent such a thing, will crush it long before its plans can be car-

[1] [Italics added.]

ried out. No, Poland will never successfully resist its neighbors—if it is content to imitate them.

In national character, in form of government, in customs, in language, Poland is quite unlike its immediate neighbors, and the rest of Europe as well. Now: I should like Poland's military organization, its tactics, its discipline, to be unlike theirs too. I should like Poland to be, in all these respects, itself, not some other country; for only by being itself will it become all that it is capable of being, and draw forth from its bosom all the resources it is capable of possessing.

The most inviolable of all the laws of nature is the law of the strongest; no legislation, no constitution can exempt anyone from that law. When, therefore, you seek the means of making yourselves secure against invasion by a neighbor stronger than you, you are seeking something that does not exist; and were you ever to try your hand at conquests, or at developing offensive power, you would be committing an even greater folly. Offensive power is incompatible with your form of government. Those who will freedom must not will conquest as well.

The Romans? But they became conquerors out of necessity and, so to speak, in spite of themselves. War was a corrective measure forced on them by the peculiar vice of their constitution. They were an island of discipline in the midst of a sea of barbarism, always attacked and always victorious, and they became masters of the world by constantly defending themselves. Your situation is so different from theirs that you cannot possibly fight off even the first attacker. You will always lack offensive power; for a long while you will lack defensive power as well. But you soon will have, or rather you have already, a capacity for self-preservation that, even if you are subjugated, will assure your survival, and keep your government and your liberty alive in their true—their only—sanctuary, which is the hearts of Polish citizens.

Regular armies have been the scourge and ruin of Europe. They are good for only two things: attacking and conquering neighbors, and fettering and enslaving citizens. Since the two are equally foreign to your nature, you must renounce the means of accomplishing them. The state must not be left without defenders? That I know. But the state's true defenders are its individual citizens, no one of whom should be a professional soldier, but each of whom should serve as a soldier as duty requires. That is how they handled the military problem in Rome; that is how they handle it now in Switzerland; and that is how it should be handled in every free state—above all in Poland, which cannot afford an army of mercenaries strong enough to defend it, and must therefore find its army, as needed, among its own people. A good militia—a genuine, well-trained militia—is the only solution to your problem. It will cost the republic little. It will be ready at all times to serve the republic. And it will serve it well, because people always fight better in defense of their own than in defense of what belongs to others.

Count Wielhorski proposes that you raise one regiment per palatinate and keep all your regiments constantly readied for action. That would involve getting rid of the crown's army, or the infantry at least, as the upkeep of thirty-three regiments is, I assume, too great a burden for the republic to carry over and above the upkeep of the crown's army. Such a change, however, would have its advantages, and would, I think, be easy to bring about; but it also might prove expensive, and you will find it difficult to prevent the abuses to which it would lead. In any case, I advise you against dispersing your soldiers over the country to maintain order in the towns and villages, because that would be poor training for them. Soldiers should never be left on their own, least of all professional soldiers; still less should they ever be charged with any sort of policing of citizens. They should march in units and bivouack in units; they should be nothing more nor less than blind instruments in the hands of their officers—always obedient, constantly under command. Even the mildest police function you might entrust to them would result in acts of violence, irritations, and abuses on a tremendous scale; in due course your soldiers and your citizens would become enemies—a misfortune that accompanies regular troops everywhere; and your constantly-mobilized regiments would unavoidably take on the cast of mind, never favorable to freedom, that is characteristic of such armies. The Roman republic was destroyed by its legions precisely when its conquests in remote places obliged it to keep them constantly on a war footing. The Poles, I repeat, should not look beyond their frontiers and imitate the things they see—not even the good things. Those things are good relative to constitutions unlike yours and would be bad under yours. The Poles should ignore what others are doing, and seek only what suits them.

The expense of regular armies outweighs a hundred times their usefulness to any people not bent upon conquests. Why not, then, do exactly what they have done in Switzerland, and give yourselves, instead, a genuine militia? There every male inhabitant is a soldier, though only when he is needed as one. The fact that serfdom exists among you does, I grant, make impossible the immediate arming of your peasants, since weapons in slavish hands will always be more dangerous than useful to the state. Pending, however, the happy moment when your serfs will be enfranchised, Poland has countless towns, whose inhabitants, once organized into regiments, could furnish, as they might be needed, large numbers of troops, whose upkeep would cost the state nothing when they were not needed. The inhabitants, for the most part, own no land, and those who do not would pay their taxes in this way. The service could, moreover, easily be shared among them in such fashion as to constitute no great burden, and yet keep them adequately trained.

In Switzerland, every bridegroom must have his uniform (it forthwith becomes the suit he wears on feast-days), his regulation rifle, and the full equipment of a foot-soldier. He is at once enrolled in the local company of the militia. In the summertime, on Sundays and on feast-days, he and his fellows are put through drills in accordance with the schedules for the several rosters—first by small squads, then by companies, then by regiments. Later, again by turns, they all go into the field

and set up small encampments, where they are drilled in all
kinds of infantry maneuvers. So long as a man does not leave
his place of abode, and there is little or no interference with
his work, he draws no pay; but when he is ordered into the
field he goes on rations and is paid by the state. No one is
permitted to send along a substitute, the idea being for each
man to receive training and perform his tour of duty.

In a state like Poland, with vast provinces to draw on, you
could easily keep enough militiamen on a war footing to take
the place of the crown's army. If each militiaman were relieved after a year's service, or perhaps even less, and if they
were called up in small detachments drawn from the various
corps, the individual burden—since a man's turn to serve
would hardly come oftener than every twelve or fifteen
years—would be small. Under such a plan, you would have a
nation of trained soldiers and a fine big army whenever you
needed it; and the latter, particularly in peacetime, would cost
much less than the crown army costs at present.

In order to succeed in this venture, however, you would
have to effect a change in public attitudes toward soldiers with
an eye to their wholly new status. That would mean seeing to
it that people think of the soldier as a citizen who is serving his
fatherland and performing his duty, and not, any longer, as a
bandit who sells himself for five sous a day to keep body and
soul together. That would restore him to the position of honor
in the community that he held in days past, and holds today in
Switzerland and Geneva. There the leading burghers are no
less proud when with their corps, under arms, than when they
are attending the sovereign council at the city hall.

You must see to it, for that purpose, that the selection of
officers goes forward without regard to birth, position, wealth,
or anything else except experience and ability. Skill with
weapons, for example, can quite easily be built up into a genuine distinction, both in the soldier's own eyes and in those of
his family, that will make each citizen throw himself zealously
into training for the service of the fatherland—as riff-raff,
recruited just anyhow, never will, because they regard training

merely as a chore. I have seen the time, in Geneva, when the burghers showed much greater skill in maneuvers than the regulars; but magistrates, feeling that the burghers were becoming imbued with a military spirit not to their liking, took steps to eliminate such rivalry—and succeeded only too well.

In putting the above plan into effect, you would be quite safe in granting your king the military authority that naturally attaches to his position. For this reason: it is not conceivable—or at least will not be when all your nationals have been given their share of liberty—that the nation could be used as an instrument for its own oppression. The executive power can enslave the state only where it has constantly-mobilized regular troops at its disposal. In Rome, for example, huge armies did no harm until they ceased to be relieved upon the naming of a new consul; until the time of Marius, indeed, it never so much as occurred to any consul that he could use them as a means of dominating the republic. But when conquests in distant places obliged the Romans to keep the same armies mobilized over a long period, to recruit vagabonds to serve in them, and to leave them indefinitely at the command of the same proconsuls, the latter began to feel independent and sought to use them for the purpose of establishing themselves in power. The armies of Sulla, Pompey, and Caesar developed into regular armies in the strict sense of the term, and acquired, in place of the state of mind appropriate to a republic, one appropriate to a military regime—to such an extent, indeed, that Caesar's soldiers felt deeply offended, on a certain occasion when he and they were displeased with one another, because he addressed them as *quirites*, that is, citizens. Under the plan I envisage, and shall soon have set forth completely, all Poland will be armed and ready to defend its liberty—alike against encroachments by the prince and against encroachments by neighboring countries. With the plan fully in effect you could—I venture to say—abolish the post of commander-in-chief, and restore its functions to the crown, without endangering your liberty in the slightest—unless the nation lets itself be inveigled into schemes of conquest, in which case I should no longer be willing to answer for the consequences. He who tries to take away the freedom of others nearly always ends up losing his own. That is true even for kings, and still more true for peoples.

It is in the knightly order that your republic in fact resides. Why, then, should it not follow some plan like the one I am proposing for the infantry? Create corps of cavalry in each palatinate. Let these corps recruit the entire nobility. Let each corps have its own officers, its own staff, and its own standard. Let each be assigned a sector for which it is to be responsible when an alarm is sounded. Let each assemble in its sector at fixed intervals during every year, so that your brave nobles can be drilled in maneuvering by squadrons and in executing all manner of movements and formations. Let them learn to put order and precision into their maneuvers. Let them learn military discipline. As for their tactics, I should by no means wish these to be modelled slavishly upon those of other nations. They should invent tactics of their own, calculated to develop and make the most of their native Polish qualities. Let them, above all, acquire swiftness and mobility; let them learn to break formation, disperse, and regroup without effort or confusion; let them excel at what is called guerilla warfare and at all the maneuvers appropriate to fast-moving units—sweeping over a countryside like a torrent, striking simultaneously at many points without ever being struck at, acting always in concert even when separated from one another, cutting communications and intercepting convoys, attacking the enemy's rearguard and isolating his vanguard, taking detachments by surprise, harassing large contingents of troops that march and camp as a body. Let them imitate the style—as they have already imitated the bravery—of the ancient Parthians. And let them learn, as the Parthians did, to defeat and destroy even the most disciplined army without ever joining battle, and without giving that army even a moment's breathing-spell. In a word, have your infantry, because you cannot do without it. But count only on your cavalry—and omit nothing that might help you invent a type of fighting that would place the outcome of any war entirely in its hands.

Fortified places are unsuited to your national character, and their maintenance is bad policy for a free people. Everywhere, soon or late, they become breeding-grounds for tyrants. The places you think you are making strong against the Russians, you will unavoidably make strong for the Russians. And those places will become shackles that you will never shake off. You should even forego any advantage you might derive from outposts, and should not bleed yourselves in order to buy artillery. That sort of thing is not what you need at all. A sudden invasion is a great calamity? Undoubtedly; but permanent chains are a far greater one. Do what you may, it will always be easy for your neighbors to penetrate your territory. You can, however, make it hard for them to get back out unscathed, and that is the objective on which you should concentrate all your efforts. Anthony and Crassus found it easy to penetrate the territory of the Parthians—but they did it to their sorrow. A vast country like yours offers its inhabitants numerous hiding places, and great facilities for slipping through an aggressor's fingers; and while all the art known to man cannot possibly prevent sudden action by the strong against the weak, that art can mobilize the forces needed for counterattack. Nor is that all: once other nations have learned by experience how costly it is to withdraw from your territory, they will be less eager to enter it. Leave the country wide open, as they did in Sparta; but build yourselves —again like Sparta—strong citadels in the hearts of your citizens. When the need arises, carry your towns on the backs of your horses, as Themistocles carried Athens on his ships. The spirit of imitation, however, produces few good things and no great ones. Each country has advantages that are its very own, and that its institutions should extend and foster. Husband and cultivate Poland's, and Poland will have few nations to envy.

One thing is enough to make Poland impossible to subjugate namely, love of the fatherland and of liberty, quickened from day to day by the virtues that always accompany it. You have just set an unforgettable example of that love; and while it may not save you from bowing briefly under the yoke, it will, if it keeps on burning in your hearts, burst into flame one day, rid you of the yoke, and make you free. To work, then, with all your zeal and with never a moment's pause, to raise each Polish heart to the highest level of patriotism!

I have already mentioned several measures calculated to accomplish that objective. But it remains for me to develop the one that I deem soundest, most efficacious, and, if properly executed, absolutely certain to succeed. It consists in seeing to it that every citizen shall feel the eyes of his fellow-countrymen upon him every moment of the day; that no man shall move upward and win success except by public approbation; that every post and employment shall be filled in accordance with the nation's wishes; and that everyone—from the least of the nobles, or even the least of the peasants, up to the king himself, if that were possible—shall be so completely dependent upon public esteem as to be unable to do anything, acquire anything, or achieve anything without it. The resulting emulation among all the citizens would produce a ferment that, in its turn, would awaken that patriotic fervor which raises men—as nothing else can raise them—above themselves. And liberty, where such patriotic fervor is absent, is merely an empty name, and laws are nothing but a mirage.

Within your knightly order, at least, you can easily establish such a system as I have in mind; you have only to take steps to apply to everything within that order the principle of step-by-step promotion, and to admit no one to honors and preferments in the state who has not previously passed through all the lower grades, each of which will thus serve both as an approach to and a test for those further on. Equality among the members of the nobility being one of Poland's fundamental laws, a career as a public servant should invariably begin in the lower grades. That is the spirit of your constitution.

The lower grades should be open to every citizen who, deeming himself capable of filling them well, has the kind of zeal that drives him to become a candidate. In any case, they should be the indispensable first step for everyone, great or small, who wishes to win advancement in the public service. Let each citizen, by all means, feel free not to present himself; but once he has become a candidate, let him, unless he himself elects to withdraw, either move up the ladder or, having been weighed in the balance and found wanting, be turned back. And let him be conscious always that every detail of his conduct is being observed and evaluated by his fellow-citizens, that no step he takes will go unnoticed, that no action he performs will be disregarded, and that the good and the evil he does are being posted upon a scrupulously accurate balance-sheet that will affect every subsequent moment of his life.

XIII

PLAN
FOR STEP-BY-STEP
PROMOTION
FOR ALL MEMBERS
OF THE GOVERNMENT

Here, now, is my proposal for a system of graduated promotions, which I have tried to adapt as much as possible to your established form of government. I assume the latter to have been reformed only with respect to the nomination of senators, in the manner, and for the reasons, set forth above.

All active members of the republic, that is, those who are to take part in its government, will be divided into three classes, each of which will have a distinctive emblem that its members will wear on their persons. Knighthoods, which in the past testified to the virtue of their recipients, are today merely evidences of royal favor; and the ribbons and jewels that are their insignia have overtones of finery and womanish adornment that we must avoid in the institution we are creating. I should like the emblems of our three orders to be struck out of distinct metals, whose intrinsic value would be in inverse proportion to the wearer's rank.

Each young man, before taking his first step upward in the public service, is to go through a period of probation: as an advocate, an assessor, perhaps even a judge, in a lower court, or as an administrator responsible for some aspect of public finance—in a word, as the incumbent of any subordinate post that offers an opportunity to demonstrate worth, ability, thoroughness, and, above all, integrity. This period of probation should not be less than three years, at the end of which he is to present himself, bearing certificates from his superiors and evidence of the public's verdict upon his performance, before the dietine of his province. That body, if after a stiff inquiry into his behavior it judges him worthy, will honor him with a shield of gold, bearing his name, the name of his province, the date of his admission, and, at the bottom, in larger characters, the legend *Spes patriae*. Those who have received this shield will wear it, either on the right arm or over the heart, at all times, and will be addressed as "servants of the state"; and only members of the knightly order who are servants of the state will be eligible to serve as deputies in the Diet, as deputy-judges of the Tribunal, or as commissioners in the Chamber of Accounts, or to perform any public function relating to the exercise of sovereignty.

Candidates for the second grade must be able to point to three terms of service as a deputy, each terminating in a vote of confidence from their constituents in the dietine; indeed, no one must be permitted to serve a second or third term in the Diet without such a vote of confidence from his dietine for his previous mandate. Service as a deputy-judge on the Tribunal or as a commissioner or deputy at Radom will be received as the equivalent of service as a deputy in the Diet; which is to say that three terms of approved service, however distributed among the three bodies, will suffice to establish a man's right to the second grade. In a word: any servant of the state who presents to the Diet the three necessary certificates will be honored with the second shield, and the title it carries with it.

This shield, which will be of the same shape and size as the first, will be struck out of silver and will bear the same inscription—except for the two words *Spes patriae*, which will be replaced by *Civis electus*. Those who wear it will be addressed as "citizens-elect," or simply "elected ones," and will no longer be eligible as mere deputies, deputy-judges of the

Tribunal, or commissioners in the Chamber of Accounts. Rather, they will be candidates for seats in the senate—to which they alone, having been admitted to the second grade and worn its emblem, will be deemed eligible. All senator-deputies will thus be drawn directly from among the citizens-elect and will continue to wear the silver shield until they achieve the third grade.

I would like you to choose the principals of your colleges and the inspectors of your primary schools from this second grade. You might, indeed, require each citizen-elect, before his elevation to the senate, to fill one of these posts for a certain period of time and duly present to the Diet his certificate of approval from the board of educational administrators. Here also, let us remember, the certificate must undergo scrutiny by the public, whom there are countless methods of consulting.

Senator-deputies will be elected at each regular session of the Diet and therefore will hold office for only two years. If, however, they receive a certificate of approval from the Diet, similar to the dietine certificate required for election to a second or third term as deputy, that will entitle them to continuance or re-election after their first and second terms of office. No one will be able to obtain a new post of any kind unless he has one of these documents to show for each function he has performed; and the man to whom one has been denied will, in order not to be excluded from the government, have to start all over again in the lower grades. That, however, he should be permitted to do, lest any zealous citizen, whatever fault he may have committed, be deprived of the hope of living it down and making a career. And let me add: the granting or refusal of the certificates should never be entrusted to committees; the decisions must be those of the chamber as a whole. Nor need this involve much inconvenience or loss of time, provided you use, for passing judgment on senator-deputies whose terms are expiring, the system of cardboard ballots that I have recommended for their election.

Someone may object at this point: all these certificates of approval, granted first by this or that agency, then by the dietines, then by the Diet, are less likely to be duly awarded to the worthy, the just, and the truthful than to be extorted by the wily and the well-connected. To that I have only one answer: I assumed, in making the proposal, that I was addressing myself to a people that, though not wholly free from vices, still possesses some energy and certain virtues; and the proposal is, on that assumption, a good one. But, if Poland has, in this regard, already reached a point where all is deep-seated venality and corruption, then it can only fail in its attempt to reform its laws and retain its liberty; it should abandon the whole venture and bow its head under the yoke. But let us return to my project.

Every senator-deputy who has successfully completed a third term will be admitted as a matter of right to the third grade, that is, the highest rung on the ladder of public service; and the shield that corresponds to it will be conferred on him, on nomination by the Diet, by the king. It will be of blue steel, and like the other two except that it will bear the inscription *Custos legum*. The man who receives it will wear it the rest of his life, no matter how exalted the posts to which he may subsequently rise, and even on the throne, should it ever befall him to ascend it.

New paladins and grand castellans will be drawn exclusively from among these "guardians of the laws," in the same way in which the latter will have been drawn from among the citizens-elect—that is, through election by the Diet. Now: the paladins will occupy the most eminent posts in the republic, and for life, and will see nothing above them except the throne; so that, in order to keep the spirit of emulation alive in them, we must open up for them an avenue to the throne itself, but in such fashion that, here also, none shall succeed save by the practice of virtue and with public approval.

Let us, before proceeding further, notice this about the road along which I have the citizens move a step at a time toward the most exalted post in the republic. It seems to be quite well adjusted to the rhythm of a human life, so that those who hold the reins of government will have left behind them the impetuosity of youth but will still be in the prime of life. After his fifteen or twenty years of testing under constant public scrutiny, a man will still have ahead of him a considerable number of years, during which the fatherland may enjoy the benefits of his talents, his experience, and his virtues, and he may enjoy, in the highest posts of the realm, the respect and honors he has so richly deserved. Suppose a man begins to find his way into public life at the age of twenty. By the time he is thirty-five he might, conceivably, have become a paladin, although it will be difficult, and even inadvisable, for a man to cover the various stages of the road thus rapidly, and he will hardly achieve that high an office before the age of forty. And forty, to my mind, is the age at which a man is most likely to combine within himself all the qualities one should look for in a statesman. Let us notice this also: the upward journey is timed so as to fit in nicely with the needs of the government. On my estimate of the probabilities, you would have, every two years, at least fifty new citizens-elect and twenty new guardians of the laws—more than enough to fill any vacancies in the two parts of the senate to which these two grades are stepping-stones. For while there will no doubt be more senators of the higher category, the vacancies there, because of life-tenure, will evidently be less frequent than vacancies in the lower category, which according to my project will be filled afresh at each regular session of the Diet.

We have already seen, and shall soon see again, that I do not leave the surplus citizens-elect idle whilst they await their call to the senate as senator-deputies. So too with the surplus guardians of the laws: in order not to leave them idle through the waiting-period before they go back to the senate as paladins or castellans, I should go to them for members of the board of educational administrators that I have mentioned above. You might make the primate, or some other bishop, chairman of this board, provided you stipulate that no other ecclesiastic, even if he is both a bishop and a senator, shall sit on it.

There, in my opinion, you have a sufficiently well-graduated system of promotion for the essential middle part of the republic, that is, for the nobles and the officials. It now remains for us to speak of the two extremes, namely, the people and the king. Let us begin with the first, which up to the present time has counted for nothing but which must, in the long run, count for something if you wish to give Poland a certain degree of strength and stability. Nothing could be more delicate than the operation in question, and, ultimately, for this reason: everyone knows how hurtful it is to the republic if the nation is in a sense confined within the knightly order, and if the remainder, that is, the peasants and burghers, have no part whatever in government and legislation. That, however, is Poland's ancient constitution, and it would be neither possible nor prudent, at the present moment, to change everything in that constitution at one and the same time. But it might be both possible and prudent to bring about, by degrees, the change here in question—that is, to see to it, without any perceptible revolution, that the most numerous part of the nation shall be tied to your fatherland, and even to your form of government, by bonds of affection. This you will accomplish in two ways: First, by scrupulously observing the principles of justice, so that the serf and the yeoman, never having any reason to fear that they will be unjustly harassed by the noble, will be cured of their present quite natural aversion to him. This calls for a drastic reform of your tribunals and for special attention to the training of your corps of advocates.

Second—and in the absence of this measure the first is useless—by opening up for the serfs a path to freedom and for the burghers a path to the nobility. Even if this is not feasible in your present situation, you must at least treat it as potentially feasible in the future. But you can go even further, in my opinion, without incurring any danger. Here, for instance, is a measure that seems to me to lead, with complete safety, in the desired direction.

Every two years, in the interval between Diets, each province would set a convenient time and place for an assembly of all its citizens-elect not yet senator-deputies. This assembly, under the presidency of a guardian of the laws not yet a senator for life, would sit as a board of censors, or board of welfare, to which it would invite not all village priests, but such village priests as might be deemed most worthy of that honor. I believe, indeed, that the fact of choosing some only among the entire number would constitute, in the eyes of the people, a tacit judgment upon them, and, by kindling in them a spirit of emulation, might rescue many of them from the dissolute way of life to which they are only too prone.

This assembly, which could also call before it elders and community leaders of every rank, would conduct hearings on proposals for improvements within the province; it would listen to reports from the priests on conditions in their own and neighboring parishes; and it would receive testimony from local leaders concerning the state of farming and family-life in their respective cantons. These reports, to which each member of the board would be free to add any comments he might wish to make, would be painstakingly verified; and a complete record would be kept of the proceedings, brief extracts of which could be furnished to the dietines.

These boards would conduct detailed inquiries into the needs of overburdened families, invalids, widows, and orphans and would provide for them, in proportion to their urgency, out of funds contributed voluntarily by the well-off. The contributions to this fund would be the less burdensome because the time would come when there would be no other gifts to charity, as neither beggars nor charitable institutions should be tolerated anywhere on Polish soil. Your priests, no doubt, will set up a hue and cry in favor of preserving the charitable institutions. But that hue and cry is merely a further reason for getting rid of them.

These boards, which would in no circumstances concern themselves with reprimands or punishments but only with benefactions, awards, and commendations, would also draw up accurate and complete lists of persons of all ranks who had so conducted themselves as to merit some distinction or reward. In drawing up these lists, the boards should look much more to the agents than to the isolated deeds.[1] The truly good deed is that done with little display. Sustained day-to-day behavior, the virtues a man practices in his private and domestic life, the faithful discharge of the duties that attach to a man's station, the actions that flow from a man's character and his principles—these are the things for which a man deserves to be honored, rather than the spectacular feats he performs only on occasion—which, for the rest, will already have had their reward in public admiration. Sensation-mongering philosophers have a great fondness for deeds that make noise; but the man with five or six such deeds to his credit, brilliant and conspicuous and widely-praised, seeks only to throw people off the scent about what he is up to—so that, with impunity, he can be unjust and hard all the rest of his life. "Give us your great deeds in small coins." This epigram, which comes to us from a woman, is very much to the point.[2]

The aforementioned lists would be forwarded to the senate and to the king, to be consulted by them, as needed, in order for them to make wise choices as regards appointments and promotions. Similarly, the reports of the boards of welfare should guide the educational administrators in awarding the scholarships that I mentioned above.

The principal and most important function of these boards, however, would be to draw up—with complete evidence, including the carefully verified verdict of public opinion—a roster of the peasants who have distinguished themselves by their good behavior, their husbandry, their manners, their devotion to their families, and their faithful discharge of the duties of their station. This roster would subsequently be presented to the dietine, which would select from it a legally-specified number of peasants to be enfranchised, and would provide, in line with procedures already agreed upon, for the compensation—by means of exemptions,

---

[1] [This sentence, and the remainder of the paragraph, appear as a footnote in the original.]

[2] [End of Rousseau's footnote.]

privileges, and other benefits in proportion to the number of their serfs found worthy of enfranchisement—of the owners. You must see to it, without fail, that the enfranchisement of the serfs shall bring honor and advantages to the masters, and not prove burdensome to them. And, in order to avoid abuses, the acts of enfranchisement would not be left up to the masters, but to the dietines, with each case being decided on its merits, and the number of cases being held within the limits set by the law.

Once you have enfranchised, one after another, a certain number of families in this or that canton, whole villages might be freed; these could then be built up little by little into communes, and assigned property and communal landholdings like those in Switzerland; communal officials could be provided for them; and, having moved things along, gradually, to the point where you could take the big step without any perceptible revolutionary change, you could concede them the right, already conferred upon them by nature, to participate in the government of their country by sending deputies to the dietines. And that step would be followed, in due course, by arming the peasants thus become freemen and citizens, organizing them into regiments, and training them. In the end you would have a first-rate militia, more than equal to the defense of the fatherland.

You could adopt a similar plan for the ennoblement of a certain number of burghers—or even, without ennobling them, set aside for them certain conspicuous public posts for which, henceforth, only they, to the exclusion of the nobles, would be eligible. Here the example has been set for you by the Venetians: though very jealous for their nobility, they reserve for their plain citizens not only certain minor offices, but also the second highest post in the government, namely, that of grand chancellor—to which, accordingly, no patrician can ever aspire. If you did likewise, throwing open to your burghers an avenue leading to ennoblement and honors, you would tie their affections both to the fatherland and to the maintenance of the constitution. Still again: without ennobling individuals, you could ennoble, collectively, certain towns, giving preference to those in which commerce, industry, and the arts had flourished conspicuously—those, that is to say, with the best municipal administration. The ennobled towns would be permitted, after the fashion of the imperial cities, to send deputies to the Diet; and their example would not fail to awaken in other towns a keen desire to win this same honor.

The boards of censors would thus be responsible for the entire department of public welfare—for which, to the shame of both kings and peoples, no provision has ever been made anywhere. Though not elective, the boards would be so constituted as to perform their functions with both zeal and integrity; their members, all of them aspirants to the senate seats corresponding to their grade, would make it their business to deserve, through public approbation, the necessary votes in the Diet; nor is anything further needed to keep them on their toes and under public scrutiny during the intervals between their terms of office. Note, however, that this would be accomplished without their ceasing to be, during the intervals, plain citizens of a certain rank. This kind of tribunal, though valuable and deserving of respect for the reasons I have stated, would have no function other than that of doing good; it would, therefore, be vested with no coercive power. In making this proposal, then, I am not increasing the total number of officials. I am merely taking advantage, as I go along, of the interval between offices, so as to get the most out of your officeholders.

Under this plan—graduated in terms of an upward movement that can be speeded up, slowed down, or even brought to a stop, according as it succeeds or fails—you would press forward no more rapidly than, guided by experience, you might wish. You would kindle, in the members of all the subordinate ranks, a burning zeal to contribute to the public good. And you would succeed, finally, in bringing to life every part of the Polish nation; you would bind all the parts together in such fashion that they would constitute a single body, whose strength and vigor would be at least ten times what it can be today. And all that with the further inestimable advantage of having avoided any change of a sudden or hasty character and all the danger that attaches to revolutions.

You have today a handsome opportunity to inaugurate this plan in an impressive and noble manner, which should produce the greatest possible effect. The Confederates, in the course of the evil days Poland has just lived through, must surely have received assistance and proofs of devotion from some of the burghers, and even from some of the peasants. Imitate the magnanimity of the Romans, careful as they were, following each of the great calamities in the history of their republic, to shower proofs of their gratitude upon those who, during the crisis, had rendered them outstanding services: foreigners, Roman subjects, slaves, animals even. To solemnly confer nobility upon those burghers and freedom upon those serfs—what a fine beginning that would be! You should spare nothing in the way of pomp and display that might make the ceremony more august, more moving, and more memorable. Nor must you stop at that: the men so distinguished should remain, throughout their lives, the favorite sons of the fatherland; you should watch over them, protect them, help them, support them—even if they happen to be scoundrels. Whatever the cost, you must see to it that they prosper as long as they live—to show all Europe, by means of an example thrust under people's very noses, what the man who dares to help Poland in its hour of trial can expect from it in its hour of triumph.

Here you have, then, a rough idea, which I offer merely by way of illustration, of the means by which you can make sure that each person shall see before him an open road, always beckoning him to proceed yet further; that everyone, by serving the fatherland well, shall move gradually toward the posts of highest honor; and that virtue shall force the doors that fortune has seen fit to lock.

But I am not yet done, and the part of my plan that I have still to explain is undoubtedly the most troublesome and difficult, since it attempts to surmount obstacles against which the skill and wisdom of the most consummate statesmen have battered in vain. I am convinced, however, assuming adoption both of the above plan and the very simple measure I am about to propose—that all difficulties will disappear, all abuses will be forestalled, and what appeared to be a further obstacle will, at the moment of execution, turn into an advantage.

XIV

ELECTING THE KING

All the aforementioned difficulties resolve themselves into one: how to give the state a chief whose mode of selection produces no civil strife and who will strike no blow at freedom. And what increases the difficulty is this: that chief should possess all the great qualities that are indispensable to the man who undertakes to govern free men. A hereditary crown prevents civil strife but leads to slavery. An elective crown safeguards freedom but shakes the state to its foundations at the beginning of every reign. The dilemma is disagreeable; but before we discuss the means of escaping between its horns, perhaps you will permit me a moment's reflection on the manner in which the Poles normally handle the succession to the crown.

The first question I should like to ask is: Why must they always give themselves kings who are foreigners? What peculiar blind spot has made them cling to the surest means of enslaving their country, of uprooting their customs, of making themselves the plaything of foreign courts, and of magnifying the confusion of their interregna? What an injustice to themselves! What an affront to the fatherland! As if, having despaired of finding in their own bosom a man worthy to lead them, they were obliged to seek him abroad! How is it their hearts have never told them, how is it their eyes have never seen, that it is precisely the other way 'round? Scan the annals of your nation: you will find it illustrious and triumphant only under Polish kings, almost always oppressed and degraded under foreign ones. Let experience come at last to the aid of reason, and open your eyes to the evils you visit upon yourselves, and the advantages you deny yourselves.

And I ask further: How is it that Poland, having done so much to keep its crown elective, has never thought of turning its law of succession to good purpose, so as to stir up in its public servants a spirit of mutual emulation in zeal and glorious achievement—which emulation alone would have accomplished more for the good of the country than all other laws put together. For men of great heart and ambition, what a powerful magnet it would be, that crown, if reserved for the most worthy, if held up constantly before the eyes of every citizen capable of deserving public esteem! What virtues, what inspired acts of devotion, might you not evoke in your people if every man could hope, by means of them, to win this highest of prizes! What a ferment of patriotism you might stir up in every heart, if all knew that only by patriotism could a man win this exalted post, transformed now into the secret object of everyone's desires—if all knew that it would depend on each man alone whether, through merit and service, he would move ever closer to the crown, and, with luck, actually make it his own. Let us seek the best means of setting this magnet, so potent in any republic and so neglected hitherto, to work! And if someone objects that merely reserving the crown for Poles is not going to get us around all the difficulties, I answer: We shall see about that in a moment, as soon as I have completed my proposal. The expedient I have in mind is simple, though when I say that it introduces the casting of lots into the procedure for electing the king, it will at first seem to fail the very purpose I have myself just stressed. I beg my readers to kindly allow me time to explain myself, or simply to re-read carefully what I have to say.

Someone may ask: How make sure that a king selected by lot will possess the qualities he needs in order to discharge worthily the duties of his office? This is an objection that I have already taken care of: you have only to see to it that no one can be elected king except senators-for-life, who will themselves be drawn from the order of guardians of the laws, and will have passed with honor through each of the republic's grades. The testing of a lifetime in all the posts they will have filled, along with the approval of the public, will be all the guarantee you need of their merit and virtue.

Nevertheless, I do not propose, even with the drawing limited to life-tenure senators, to have chance alone determine the result; that would be to fall still short of the grand objective that you should set yourselves. A little must be left up to chance, but a great deal to choice, so as to seal off the intrigues and plots of foreign powers, and also to bind each of the paladins, by direct personal interest, to keep his conduct up to the mark and continue to serve the fatherland with zeal in order to deserve preference over his rivals.

I do grant this: the group of competitors will be rather large—if we include in it the grand castellans, who under the existing constitution are approximately equal in rank to the paladins. But I do not see any objection to reserving direct access to the throne for the paladins. That would create, within one and the same order, a further upward step, which the grand castellans would have to take in order to become paladins, and thus a further means of keeping the senate dependent upon the legislator. As the reader already knows, I consider the grand castellans a superfluity in your constitution; in order to avoid any great change, however, let them retain both their posts and their seats in the senate. But in the graduated scheme I propose there is nothing that either requires or prevents their being placed on the same level as the paladins; and you will be able, without difficulty, to adopt whichever course seems better to you. But I assume, for purposes of this discussion, that you will choose to give the paladins alone direct access to the throne.

Immediately after the death of the king—that is, after the

briefest possible legally-stipulated interval—the electoral Diet will be solemnly convoked. The names of all the paladins will be entered upon the lists and, with every possible precaution against fraudulent manipulation of the drawings, three of them will be drawn by lot. These three names will then be read out to the assembly, and the latter, in that selfsame session and by majority vote, will elect the one of the three whom it prefers. And the man so chosen will be proclaimed king that very day.

Some readers, I realize, will feel that this electoral procedure has one great drawback, namely, this: the nation cannot choose freely, among the paladins, that one whom it most honors and cherishes, and deems most worthy of the kingship. This drawback, however, will be no novelty in Poland. In several of its elections, the most recent especially, we have seen it forced, without regard to the candidates the nation favored, to elect someone whom it would have liked to send packing. And in return for this advantage, which it no longer enjoys and which it gives up, how many greater advantages it acquires through this form of election!

First of all, the drawing of lots puts an end, once and for all, to combines and intrigues on the part of foreign powers, which cannot influence this kind of election and are too uncertain of the issue to expend much effort on it; since the nation can always reject any of the winners, a fraud perpetrated in behalf of one of them will not, in itself, turn the trick. This gain alone is sufficient to assure Poland peace and quiet, stamp out venality in the republic, and surround the election with a tranquillity approaching that of hereditary monarchy.

There is the same advantage as regards intrigues on the part of the candidates themselves. Which of them is going to lay out money in the attempt to make sure of a nomination that no man can control? Which of them, with the odds of the event so overwhelmingly against him, is going to throw away his fortune on it? To which let us add: those whom chance favors will not have time to buy up votes, since the balloting takes place then and there.

The nation's free choice among three candidates protects

it from the untoward consequences of any drawing in which—for let us assume that might happen—an unworthy man is successful, for it will take care not to elect him. And for three unworthy men to be successful in a drawing among thirty-three illustrious citizens, the elite of the nation, is unthinkable, since it is hard to see how a single unworthy man could be found in such a company.

In a word—and I attach great weight to this observation—we bring together, under this scheme, all the advantages of both hereditary monarchy and elective monarchy.

For, to begin with, the crown will never pass from father to son, so that there will be none of that continuity of system which might bring about the republic's enslavement. And, secondly, chance itself operates in the scheme as a means to a free and enlightened electoral choice. For it can make no selection, from among this venerable body of guardians of the laws and paladins drawn from their number, that has not been made at an earlier date by the nation itself.

Just think of the spirit of emulation that this prospect will introduce into the order of the paladins and grand castellans. All of them, what with their life-tenure, what with their certain knowledge that their offices cannot be taken away from them, might cease to exert themselves. Fear can no longer hold them in line. But the hope of ascending a throne, which each of them can see an arm's length ahead of him, is a fresh incentive, nicely calculated to keep them always on their toes. All of them know that fortune will smile on them in vain if rejection awaits them at the balloting stage, and that the only way to get themselves elected is to deserve to be elected. Your own gain is so great and obvious that I need not insist upon it.

Let us suppose, however, that worst comes to worst, that you cannot prevent fraud in the drawing, and that one of the participants succeeds in cheating the vigilance of the others, deeply interested though they are in the outcome. The fraud will of course hurt the candidates whom it puts out of the running; but the consequences for the republic will be what they would have been if the lots had been cast fairly: all the advantages of an elective monarchy, and none of the turmoil of the interregna, none of the dangers attaching to a hereditary succession. More: the candidate whose personal ambition has tempted him to resort to fraud will not, on this account, be any the less a man of merit in other respects, capable, in the nation's judgment, of wearing the crown with honor. Nor, finally, once the fraud has been perpetrated, will he stand any the less in need, as far as profiting from it is concerned, of the subsequent formal election by the republic.

Once all the phases of my plan have been put into effect, everything will be tied into the state, and no one, from the most obscure private citizen up to the ranking paladin, will see before him any path to advancement other than that of duty and public acclaim. Only the king, once he is elected and has above him nothing except the laws, has no brake upon him apart from the laws; he alone, having nothing further to gain from public approbation, is able, when his plans so require, to cut himself off from it without risk. I see hardly any way of meeting this problem except one that we must not even think of, namely, to make it possible, in some fashion, to unking the king and to require him to be confirmed in office every so many years. Such a solution, I say, is not worth proposing; it would keep both the throne and the state in constant turmoil, and would, in consequence, never afford the administration the solid base it needs if it is to devote itself exclusively and productively to the public good.

Ancient history tells of a usage, confined indeed to a single people, that was so salutary in its results that I cannot imagine why other peoples have not been tempted to imitate it, namely, the judgment that the Egyptians passed on each of their kings after he was dead, and the decree granting or denying him royal burial and honors according to his good or bad government of the state during his lifetime. Though invented and practiced by a hereditary kingdom, the usage, nevertheless, makes little sense except in an elective monarchy—for all that the idea of reviving it for the kings of

Poland may seem quite mad, and for this reason: modern men are indifferent to moral considerations and to everything capable of developing the resources of the spirit. I should not like to try to persuade some Frenchmen—especially some French philosophers—to adopt such a practice. But one can, I think, recommend it to readers in Poland; and I venture to suggest that the Poles would reap great benefits from it, the like of which they assure themselves in no other way, and without any untoward consequences. For our immediate purpose, at least this is easy to see: unless he is a low fellow, who cares not a snap of his fingers whether his memory is held in honor or not, the king cannot fail to be deeply touched by this unavoidable and impartial judgment upon his behavior. It will act as a brake upon the king's passions, more powerful no doubt with some kings than with others, but powerful enough, with every king, to hold them within certain bounds—especially if we toss into the balance the interests of their children, whose destiny will be determined by the judgment passed upon their fathers' memory.

What I propose, then, is this: after the death of a king, let his body lie in some suitable place pending the judgment upon his memory. Let the tribunal, which is to hand down the judgment and designate his place of burial, be assembled at the earliest possible moment. Let the facts concerning his life and reign be scrupulously examined: let there be hearings, in the course of which everyone must have his opportunity to speak out for or against him. And let the examination, the conduct of which would be in the hands of able men, be followed immediately by a verdict, pronounced with all possible solemnity.

In the event of a favorable verdict, let the late king be declared a good and just prince; let his name be inscribed with honor upon the roster of the kings of Poland; let his body be laid, with all appropriate pomp, in their place of burial; let the words "of glorious memory" be added to his name in all public documents and orations; let an endowment be settled upon his widow; and let his children, having been declared royal princes, enjoy throughout their lives all the advantages attaching to that title.

If, on the other hand, the late king is found to have been unjust, violent, or corrupt; if he is declared guilty of an attempt upon the people's liberties, let his memory be condemned and held up to scorn; let his body be denied its resting-place among the kings of Poland and buried without ceremony like that of a private citizen; let his name be expunged from the roster of kings; and let his children, stripped of their princely titles and the privileges these carry with them, resume the status of ordinary citizens, without special honors but also without stigma.

I should like the judgment on the king to go forward with a maximum of display. If possible, however, it should precede the election of the new king—so that the latter's influence will not affect a decision that he will have a personal interest in making less severe. I am aware that more time would be desirable, to bring hidden facts to light and have the record more carefully reviewed. If, however, the decision were delayed until after the election, I fear that this grave proceeding would become overnight an empty formality—a funeral oration in praise of the dead king, which is what would happen as a matter of course in a hereditary monarchy, rather than a rigorous and impartial judgment upon his behavior. In order, therefore, to safeguard the integrity and severity of the judgment, which would otherwise become pointless, the better course, on this occasion, would be to dispense with this or that bit of detailed information and to give greater weight to public opinion.

As for the tribunal that would hand down the decree, I should prefer that it be neither the senate, nor the Diet, nor any entity vested with governmental authority, but rather an entire class of citizens whom it would not be easy to deceive or corrupt. I should think that the *cives electi*—better informed and more experienced than the servants of the state but less interested in the result than the guardians of the laws who are already too near the throne—would be the intermediate group

too, you will always be in danger of losing your freedom so long as Russia continues to intervene in your affairs. Should you, however, succeed in forcing Russia to deal with you as power to power and not as protector to protégé, you must forthwith take advantage of the state of exhaustion in which the war with Turkey will surely leave Russia and accomplish your task before it can confuse things.

I myself attach no importance to the external security that is won by means of treaties; but your unique situation may well oblige you to avail yourselves as much as possible of that kind of support—if only to learn the intentions of those with whom you will be dealing. Apart from that, and perhaps from a few commercial treaties in times different from these, do not wear yourselves out in idle negotiations, or waste your substance on ambassadors and ministers at other courts, or rely upon alliances and treaties for anything whatever. All that is useless as regards the Christian powers: they recognize no bonds save those of self-interest; they will redeem their commitments when it is to their interest to redeem them and violate them when it is to their interest to violate them; you will be just as well off without the commitments as with them. If, again, the interest they act on were always their real interest, knowledge of what is to their advantage might enable you to predict what they are going to do. Actually, however, what determines their policy is almost never reason of state, but rather the momentary interest of some minister, some wench, some favorite, so that the motive that pushes them toward their real interests at one moment and away from them the next, is one that human wisdom has never been able to outguess. What can you count on from people who have no fixed policy and act only on fortuitous impulse? There is nothing more frivolous than the political science of courts; since it rests upon no settled principles, one can read out of it no certain consequences. And all the pretty doctrines concerning the "interests of the crown" are a child's game, at which sensible men can only laugh.

Do not, then, lean with any confidence either upon your

allies or upon your neighbors. You have only one neighbor that you can count on to some extent, namely, the sultan of Turkey, and you should spare no effort to get his support, though not because his maxims of state are notably more reliable than those of other powers. There also everything depends upon some vizir, some favorite, some harem intrigue. But Turkey's interest is obvious and simple; it is a matter of "Everything for Turkey"; and, generally speaking, its policy is more upright and sensible, if at the same time less enlightened and less adroit, than that of other powers. Moreover, one has with Turkey, as compared to the Christian powers, at least this further advantage: it likes to redeem its commitments and ordinarily respects its treaties. You should try to negotiate a Turkish treaty, as strong and clearly-worded as possible, for a period of twenty years: it will be the surest, perhaps the only guarantee that you can have whilst a certain other power keeps its intentions secret; and, given the condition in which the present war will in all likelihood leave Russia, my guess is that you need nothing more in order to undertake your reform safely. I feel this the more strongly since the European powers, and above all your other neighbors, have a common interest in seeing to it that you are always there as a barrier between themselves and Russia, and since these countries, in the course of substituting one folly for another, can hardly fail to behave wisely at least on occasion.

One thing convinces me that other powers will, in general, not bother you with their suspicions as you work away at the reform of your constitution; the reform in question tends exclusively to the strengthening of your legislature, and thus of your liberty, which is something that all courts regard as a visionary fancy that tends rather to weaken a state than to strengthen it. That is why France has always favored the liberty of the Germanic states and of Holland, and why Russia not only supports the present government of Sweden but does everything in its power to thwart the designs of the Swedish king. All these great ministers of state judge men in general by themselves and those around them and think they understand them. They do not, therefore, even begin to imagine the strength that love of fatherland and the spirit of virtue are capable of developing in the souls of free men; and when they find themselves duped by their low opinion of republics, which always put up far greater resistance to their enterprises than they expect, they learn nothing from it and will never shake off this preconception that is rooted in the contempt which they know themselves to deserve and in terms of which they evaluate all humankind. The Russians, despite the highly instructive experience they have just had in Poland, will let nothing change their opinion; they will continue to look upon free men just as one must look upon them, that is, as mere good-for-nothings who respond to only two instruments: money, and the knout. When, therefore, they see that the republic of Poland—instead of laboring to fill its coffers, expand its financial system, and recruit large numbers of regular troops—is planning to disband its army and do without money, they will think that Poland is busy weakening itself; believing that they can conquer by merely knocking at its door the day they please, they will let Poland order itself in comfort, and laugh up their sleeves at its way of going about it. For the rest, the condition of freedom does deprive a people of offensive power; in adopting the plan I propose, then, you must renounce all hope of conquests. But twenty years hence, when your reform is completed, just let the Russians have a try at invading you: they will learn soon enough how they fight in defense of their homes, these men of peace who know nothing about attacking the homes of others, and have forgotten the price of money.

One further thing: Once you have rid yourselves of those cruel visitors, beware of adopting a soft policy toward the king they have seen fit to impose upon you. You must either cut off his head, which is what he deserves, or disregard the election that brought him to the throne, which is completely invalid, and re-elect him with new *pacta conventa*, in which you must make him renounce the appointment of your high officials. The second of these two courses of action is both the more humane and the wiser. I see in it, indeed, a certain generous pride that may annoy the court of St. Petersburg quite as much as would your electing someone else. Poniatowski, in past days, was certainly a criminal through and through; today he is perhaps hardly more than an object for pity. He seems to be conducting himself, in the present situation at least, pretty much as he ought to—by keeping his nose out of everything; and it is only natural that he should yearn, deep in his heart, for the expulsion of his stern taskmasters. The part of the patriot-hero would perhaps be to join the confederates and help chase the Russians out of the country. But everybody knows that Poniatowski is no hero; and, quite apart from the fact that he has no freedom of action and is under constant surveillance, he owes everything to the Russians. The last thing I should wish for if I were in Poniatowski's shoes, I confess it frankly, would be the capacity for heroism.

I know very well that Poniatowski is not the king you will need when you have completed your reform; but he is perhaps the one you need in order to complete it without outside interference. Suppose he lives only another eight or ten years: your new system will by that time already have begun to operate; several guardians of the laws will already be paladins; you will be beyond the risk of giving him a successor who resembles him. But if you simply dethrone him, you will not, I fear, know what to do with him and will expose yourselves to further disturbances.

Whatever the difficulties you might sidestep by making him king in a free election, you must not think of such a thing until you have made certain where his real sympathies lie, and even then only if you have found in him a certain amount of good sense, of sense of honor, of love of country, along with some understanding of what the country's interests call for, and some desire to pursue them. Nothing could be more disastrous for Poland than to have a traitor at the head of its government—at any time, but especially in the sad situation in which its current misfortunes are about to leave it.

A word now about how to get your reform under way: I have no taste for the subterfuges that have been proposed for somehow taking the nation by surprise, or pulling the wool over its eyes, about the changes to be made in its laws. My advice would be merely this: reveal your plan in all its details, but do not begin its execution so brusquely as to weight the republic down with malcontents. Leave most of your officeholders in their present positions, and make no appointments under the new system save as positions become vacant. Never give your governmental system any shock that is too sudden. I feel sure that a good plan, once in effect, will touch the hearts even of those who have taken part in the government under another system. But since citizens of a new type cannot be created overnight, you must begin by getting what you can out of the citizens you have; and the way to dispose them to follow a new path is to open one up to their ambitions.

But if, despite the courage and constancy of the confederates, despite the justice of their cause, both fortune and the powers abandon them, delivering the fatherland into the hands of its oppressors—Ah, but I do not have the honor to be a Pole, and in a situation like yours one is not permitted to give advice unless by example.

I have now executed, to the best of my ability, the task entrusted to me by Count Wielhorski—with, God grant, success commensurate with my fervor. There you have my ideas, which may be nothing more than a series of idle fancies; and it is not my fault—since I have never been given the opportunity to organize my head in some other manner—if they are so little like those of other men. For all that they may seem strange to others, I see in them nothing that is not well-adapted to the human heart, and good and practicable besides—especially for Poland, since I have tried throughout to follow the spirit of the Polish republic, and to propose no changes other than those needed to remedy its defects. A government established upon such bases should, I think, move toward the accomplishment of its true purpose with a maximum of directness and certainty over a maximum period of time, though I do not forget that all human achievements are imperfect, transitory, and shortlived, even as men are.

I purposely omit many extremely important matters on

which I have not thought myself sufficiently informed to venture any judgment. I leave them to others, more enlightened and wise than I, and, with apologies to Count Wielhorski for having taken so much of his time, I bring this long, rambling discourse to a close. Though my ideas do differ from those of other men, I do not flatter myself that I am wiser than they, or that the Count will find in my reflections anything that will prove truly useful to his country. But my wishes for Poland's well-being are so genuine, so pure, and so disinterested, that pride in contributing to that well-being could add nothing to my zeal. May Poland be triumphant over its enemies; may it become—and remain—a peaceful country, happy and free; may it set a great example for the entire world; and may it, profiting from Count Wielhorski's patriotic labors, bear and suckle many citizens of his breed.

SUGGESTIONS FOR FURTHER READING

On Rousseau's *The Government of Poland:*
Anne M. Cohler, *Rousseau and Nationalism.* New York: Basic Books, 1970.
Stephen Ellenburg, *Rousseau's Political Philosophy: An Interpretation from Within.* Ithaca, N.Y.: Cornell University Press, 1976.
Richard Fralin, *Rousseau and Representation.* New York: Columbia University Press, 1978.
Those who read French should consult Jean Fabre's edition of the text, with introduction and notes, in vol. 3 of *Jean Jacques Rousseau: Oeuvres Complètes,* Eds. Bernard Gagnebin and Marcel Raymond. 4 vols. Paris: Bibliothèque de la Pléiade, 1959–69.

On Rousseau in general:
Roger D. Masters, *The Political Philosophy of Rousseau.* Princeton, N.J.: Princeton University Press, 1968.
Judith N. Shklar, *Men and Citizens; A Study of Rousseau's Social Theory.* Cambridge: Cambridge University Press, 1969.
Leo Strauss, *Natural Right and History.* Chicago: University of Chicago Press, 1953.